Journey Well

A Biblical Guide to Life's Most Practical Lessons

Mick Naples

Foreword by Edward Wilde

ISBN 978-1-7345950-0-0

Cover Design by 100Covers.com
Interior Design by FormattedBooks.com

Dedication

To my dad. Getting to this point in life and with this book would not have been possible without him. No one on earth has done more for me than that man. Even though he is gone, I continue to learn from him. If the Lord blesses me with a family of my own one day, I'll have done well if I am half the father he was to me.

Christmas, 2021

Zoe,
   This was written by a young pastor friend. He is wise for his years + I love his outlook on life + his love for Christ. love -
Omi

Acknowledgments

Because I am certain I will undervalue some important person who played some critical role in my life or in this project, I find writing this section difficult. The world's notion of the "self-made man" is a farce, and in reality, none of us ever really accomplishes anything without the help and influence of others along the way. I am grateful to God for the people He has placed in my life to get me to this point, and I want to particularly acknowledge those who played a part in this project. I again stress, though, that the help I have received and the credit that I owe could not possibly be confined to these pages.

First, I would like to thank all of the pastors (especially my own, who aside from their time spent reading through my manuscript have always been more than willing to invest in me, support me, and help me), professors, professionals, and friends who read early drafts of my manuscript. These people owed me nothing and took the time from their busy schedules to work their way through my scattered thoughts and offer their insight. In one instance, an early draft found its way into the hands of someone I didn't even know. She took the initiative to read through it and reach out to me with no small amount of encouragement. Thanks, Meg!

Next, I want to thank Pastor Joe Propri and Dr. Greg Gifford for their positive reviews of my work, along with Professor Edward Wilde for his willingness to contribute and write the magnificent foreword that now adorns the finished product. Similarly, I owe a lot to my friend Paul, who, generally speaking, has had a profound impact on the refinement of my thoughts on life and, specifically speaking, on the refinement of my thoughts in this book.

Though he is mentioned in the pages that follow, I would be remiss if I didn't acknowledge here my friend Jeff. He has been the closest of mentors and is high on the list of people who have helped me to see the world in a better way and to become a better man. I can't put a price tag on the many hours spent at his kitchen table talking about "the journey of life." Many of those sessions involved Jeff nearly beating me to death. I speak figuratively, of course, but Jeff never pulled any punches in trying to help me see my shortcomings as well as my strengths, urging me (often colorfully) to fight through the former and encouraging me to see the reality of the latter.

Jeff has a gift to see God-given potential in people and in life's situations, and he was relentless in helping me see it too. We all need friends like this if we are to become the best version of ourselves. Such a pursuit honors God because the best version of who we are is the one that looks most like Him. Since Jeff always signed off his many emails to me with the valediction, "Journey Well," I also owe him credit for the title and theme of the book. His influence in my life has been paramount, and he has truly helped me to *journey well*.

I would also like to thank my editor, Beacon Point LLC, and my proofreader, Paul Miller. They transformed my manuscript and are responsible for taming some of my verbosity and clarifying some of my ramblings. The book would certainly not be as accessible as it is without their work.

My mom and sister also need to be mentioned. They really didn't have much knowledge of this project as I was completing it (my fault, not theirs), but they have always been supportive of anything I've ever set out to accomplish.

Lastly and most importantly, I want to thank our Triune God— Father, Son, and Holy Spirit. The Father's gracious providence; the Son's life, death, and resurrection; and the Spirit's grace and guidance have all brought me to this very point in my life, and I am so incredibly grateful.

Contents

Foreword

There is a book genre that promises to teach you about topics you won't learn in school. These books promise practical knowledge, such as how to run a business, make investments, or sell a script. While school can teach us some things, these books teach "real-world" knowledge. Such books have a ready market because they offer practical, useful skills that are overlooked in traditional education.

What these books sell is niche wisdom. Wisdom is not just knowledge; it is knowledge for the real world, for day-to-day living. What you are holding in your hands is also a book on real-world wisdom, but rather than being niche wisdom for someone opening an Etsy shop, it is wisdom for life.

Mick is an educator, and in his position he saw, day by day, the limitations of schoolroom education. Mick has also received graduate education in biblical wisdom, the sort of counsel that helps for all of life. That is how I came to know Mick—as a student and as a friend. I have come to value his wisdom, and I am sure that you, too, will find this book valuable for many reasons.

We live in a world that desperately needs wisdom. We can learn much, but we know very little. Someone once quipped that on the internet we have access to more knowledge than the library of Alexandria, but we spend our time watching cat videos.

We as humans have amassed a monumental mechanism to convey data. If one lacks what is called an "education," it is not for lack of information; we are awash in facts, figures, studies, and opinions. Yet what has all this data and material well-being produced? When we look to the leaders of society, do we see people who are worthy of their position? When we look to the general population, we see the anxious and the confused. We live in a world of insanity and consumerism.

Despite all our information and education, we have not produced people who know how to live.

Years ago, a cult leader in Japan managed to gain control over well-credentialed scientists and engineers. Despite all their excellent education, they could not see through the fraud of a cult leader who led them to murder while he was wearing a pasta strainer on his head. If they were not murderous, they would be comical. They knew how to build bridges, but not how to live a life. They sought guidance on how to live at the hands of a charlatan because they had no true wisdom.

On the other end of the spectrum, a friend who is a contractor told me the story of repairing the house of a man who had become wealthy from pornography. As my friend worked, he played a reading of the Bible book Ecclesiastes. As the pornographer heard the wisdom of Solomon as he explained the vanity and emptiness of a life without God, the pornographer was transfixed. Not knowing he was hearing the Bible, the man asked, "Can you get me a copy of that?"

The Japanese engineers were looking for wisdom and found a fool. The pornographer had gained wealth and debauchery, a consumer of human life par excellence, and knew it was all vain.

We are conveying data, but no wisdom.

What we need is wisdom. We can live fulfilled lives without televisions or cellphones or automobiles, but we cannot live well without wisdom.

What Mick has done is simply provide the basics of wisdom, which so many lack.

We know that we need this sort of wisdom; hence, the rise of the life coach. Yet, as Mick explains, these coaches have nothing to answer if they only look to their own experience. We need the wisdom of someone who knows more.

I won't recount here what Mick will explain ahead. He writes with the clarity of someone who has learned to teach and with the winsome touch of a teacher who cares.

If you are a young person who is getting ready to head out into life, this book is for you. If you know some young people getting ready to head out into life, you would do a good turn by placing this book into their hands.

Edward Wilde
September 2019

Introduction

A smart man makes a mistake, learns from it, and never makes that mistake again. A wise man finds a smart man and learns from him how to avoid the mistake altogether.
—ROY H. WILLIAMS[1]

Have you ever heard the phrase, "Youth is wasted on the young"? Perhaps you hadn't, but you have now. I encourage you to spend some time thinking through this. I know I have. I was unaware of such a mantra until one Sunday morning at church when it was mentioned in a conversation I was having with a friend. If there's one thing that life has taught me over the years, it's that this statement is true. Another way to say it could be the oft-stated caveat of "If only I knew then what I know now." There are many variations of this, but hopefully by now you're starting to get my point. Youth really is wasted on the young—but why does it have to be that way?

---

1   I have tried to be thorough in my citations herein, but unfortunately I happened upon many of the quotes that made their way in here on my Facebook newsfeed or just from searching for quotes on Google or Pinterest. The many memes (that we all enjoy reading) floating around out there do not make it easy to give full citations. So in some instances, only the author has been given, and even then it was sometimes difficult to verify with certainty that the quote was attributed to the right person.

In some sense, the sense in which this entire book has been written, it doesn't have to be. But in a much more common sense, it's that way because we often don't heed the wisdom we should. Whether it's because we're literally ignorant of it, because we think we know better, or because we're "following our heart" in a different direction, the fact is that in life we often find ourselves needing to be dug out of some pretty precarious holes. Life has a way of teaching us lessons that get through to us in a way that someone's advice just can't. Experience is powerful and is often a harsh teacher, as I'm sure you can attest to in one way or another.

This book was born out of an incredible (and God-given) sense of self-awareness. To be blunt, I took a long, hard look at my life and realized I wasn't even close to where I thought I would be by now. Such a glance was the impetus for some serious reflection. It led me to really think through how I had gotten here. What had I missed? What had I done wrong? What lessons are to be learned? How does God fit into all this? And, of course, how do I fix things?

As I came to seek and find answers to all these questions, a couple of things happened. The first is that I found myself having an incredible passion to share all these lessons, all these life principles. I wanted others to learn what I had learned. It was evident, at least in my own life, that despite how clear and common many of these lessons are, applying them appropriately is anything but common.

I also realized that God Himself had taught me everything I learned. I'm making two points when I say this, and both are significant. First, God taught me these lessons because my life, including my mistakes, never ceases to be under the umbrella of His good and sovereign providence. So if you aren't exactly where you want to be in life, be encouraged. God put me in all the situations I've been in. He certainly was not culpable for any of my foolishness, any of my sinful dispositions, or any of my shortcomings, but He never ceased to work things out according to the counsel of His will (Ephesians 1:11). What a gracious act—that He would see fit to teach me! Many of the lessons were hard, costly, and painful, but I learned them nonetheless, and I was better off for having learned them. This paradigm can be seen in Hebrews 12:11: *For the moment all discipline seems painful rather than pleasant, but later it yields the peaceful fruit of righteousness to those who have been trained by it.*

Lessons are hard, but it's God's loving care that, through His providence, brings them to us. *For the Lord disciplines the one he loves, and chastises every son whom he receives* (Hebrews 12:6).

God's providence notwithstanding, I began to see something incredible about all that God was teaching me in life, which was not immediately obvious to me. I eventually realized that just about all the principles I was learning were actually found in God's Word, the Bible. That is to say, if I had been more familiar with God's teaching beforehand, I may have learned these same lessons earlier and may have been spared some of the consequences of foolish and uninformed living. Or if I had not been spared from experiences that inevitably come to us all in various forms, I would have been equipped to better and more biblically handle life as it happened—as it tends to happen to us all.

Thus, it is incumbent upon me to take up the pen (or the laptop, but I have a great appreciation for antiquity, and "pen" definitely sounds better) and share these lessons with you. In the Gospel of Mark, Jesus happens upon a group of weary and wayward-looking people, and we're told that He had compassion on them. The interesting part, though, is that the demonstration of His compassion was that *He began to teach them many things* (Mark 6:34). So, I want to teach you—not just because I'm a teacher at heart and have spent the bulk of my professional career in education, but because it's compassionate and it's what Jesus did.

My aim is not only to teach you some of the many lessons I've learned over the years, but also to provide a biblical interpretation of the experiences I know you will go through (or have gone through) as you continue this great and exciting journey called life. Although we're all unique in various ways, there really is nothing unique about the human experience (1 Corinthians 10:13). So when hardship comes, and it will come, the best way to handle it is according to the wisdom God has given us in His Word, and that's what I seek to help you do.

Since the pages that follow are a biblical interpretation of many of the lessons I've learned and situations I've experienced, some of what I reveal is very personal—and also somewhat embarrassing. But I need to be honest because that is the model I want to demonstrate for you. As Heath Lambert so well explains, as Christians, "we need to work to be the kinds of people who are honest about our own struggles"[2] (in a discerning way, of course). We should want to help people, and we should want to be the type of people whom others come to for help. Helping people in such a way goes hand in glove with being open about our struggles.

I'll never forget being open about my life with a friend from church while having coffee together, and then hearing him say, "I never knew you struggled with things like that." Up until that cup of coffee, he had primarily known me as a Sunday school teacher and as someone who occasionally filled the pulpit. Since that conversation, though, our friendship has grown and I've been in a position to help and encourage him in a few different areas of his life. More than that, he's done the same for me. Iron really does sharpen iron (Proverbs 27:17).

That relationship may have never grown if I hadn't been a little vulnerable, a little willing to share something of myself. After all, people don't generally want to open up to someone about their struggles if they think they're talking to someone who doesn't struggle himself. But the truth is that we all struggle, regardless of our gifts or our knowledge. We all need one another. This thing that God ordained—the church—has a purpose. It wasn't an accident. So even as I seek to model that herein, I encourage you to do the same in your own lives with those around you.

Additionally, I want you to be aware, as you are informed of struggles from my own life and as you interact with others, that

---

2   Heath Lambert, "Sufficiency of Scripture."(lecture, BCI Conference, North Ridgeville, OH, May 3, 2014).

suffering is very subjective in nature. What I mean is that many of you are going to read about my life and be tempted to think, *That's it? I've gone through way harder trials than that!* Well, I don't doubt that at all. In fact, I fully recognize that despite some hard lessons, God has been incredibly gracious to me and, comparatively, I haven't endured much hardship at all. Comparatively, I've had a pretty easy life. But my struggles are my own, just like yours are your own, and God uniquely uses these challenges to mold us more and more into the image of His Son (Romans 8:29; Hebrews 12:11). We should never trivialize the suffering of those around us.

Another point I'd like to make is that each chapter, although thoroughly biblical in its scope, begins with and sometimes includes quotations from non-Christian sources. I have three reasons for this. The first is plain and simple. I find them to be helpful reminders of principles I've learned in my own life.

The second reason has much to do with *why* they've been helpful, and that's because they're generally true. I want you to recognize that upholding the sufficiency of Scripture doesn't preclude us from gaining insight elsewhere. Although the Bible is sufficient for *all things that pertain to life and godliness* (2 Peter 1:3) and is the only perfect and infallible source of truth, we can learn things from non-Christian sources as well. The most obvious example I can think of is recognizing the reality that many people (myself included) have parents who aren't believers. I've learned much from them over the years. I mean they taught me how to use a fork and even how to go to the bathroom properly—skills we all have (more or less) and weren't born knowing how to do. The testimony of Scripture is that I'm foolish if I don't consider what they have to say about life.

The third reason I've included such quotations is because I want you to see the universality of God's wisdom. So true are His axioms, so wise are His precepts and principles, that even those who don't know Him in a saving way can recognize important truths about His creation and the way things work in life. Accordingly, John Calvin observes that "Whenever we come upon these matters in secular writers, let that admirable light of truth shining in them teach us that the mind of man, though fallen and perverted from its wholeness, is nevertheless clothed and ornamented with God's excellent gifts."[3]

What Calvin is saying here is that even though non-Christians are blind to ultimate truth and their hearts are hardened against their Creator, they can nonetheless observe and conclude many right and true things about the created order. Consider also that much of the wisdom from non-Christians is actually borrowed from our own worldview. Marvel at that and let it strengthen your resolve to always trust the unfailing Word of God.

What follows is a collection of so many things I wish someone had told me a long time ago. Mind you, my ignorance was my own fault (and it is never bliss), but what a great benefit it would've been to have known such things when I was younger. I would have had opportunity for so many different things. I could have lived so much more wisely and thus embraced so much more fully what God has given us to enjoy here. Alas, I was either unaware or did not pay attention to such wisdom. If you find yourself in similar shoes, remember that God is still on the throne. He has never vacated, and He never will. I'm not where I am by accident, and neither are you. You're reading this book for a reason. I'm not sure what that reason is—maybe you don't even know—but God has a purpose in it, and that is comforting. Similarly, He has a purpose in my writing it.

In short, I want to help you live. I mean to *really* live. I want to help you enjoy all that God has given you and to help you live wisely and make the most of the opportunities He might graciously provide. The world calls people who offer advice on such things "life coaches." They're everywhere. They all claim to have the answer, and many of them are making millions.

Coaches are good things. A coach is someone who is there to push you to be your best and instruct you in the proper way of

---

3   Jean Calvin and Ford L. Battles, *Calvin: Institutes of the Christian Religion* (Louisville: Westminster John Knox Press, 2001), 273.

doing something. A life coach, then, is someone who does that with aspects of life. The question for all these "life coaches" out there, and for anyone who thinks that such people have the answers to their problems, is "How on earth can anyone be coached through life without the wisdom that is found in God's Word?"

The answer is that it can't be done. Without the Bible, people miss out on the most important things—not only of this life, but in relation to the life to come as well. That's not doing any true good to anyone. Properly viewed, what the world calls "life coaching" we should look at as discipleship. That's the model God has given us—where the older and more experienced people instruct those who are younger and less experienced (Titus 2:1–8). Disciples making disciples is what we need, and it is what we're called to be. We need people willing to plumb the depths of God's Word and share the riches of wisdom therein, to look at their experiences, both good and bad, and to come to a better understanding of what God would teach us about such things.

The Bible really has practical life lessons for us and has the answers for the problems that we experience in life. John Chrysostom, who was considered the greatest preacher of the ancient world, noted that "It is possible to find in Scripture a remedy appropriate to every trouble afflicting the human race and to dispel every depression that life causes and not be brought low by any circumstance befalling us."[4] Such is my aim here: to point you to that remedy as I share my understanding of God's wisdom on many of the experiences I've faced in life, and that you will likely face too.

This book walks the tension-filled line of biblical wisdom, which is tied on one end to the reality of eternity, and is tied on the other end to practical living in the here and now. These truths are not enemies. A proper understanding of the former necessarily informs the latter. At one point in my life, I left a strictly biblical

---

4   Ed Wilde, "The Theology of Psychology" (lecture, ACBC Africa, April 7, 2017).

perspective and began exploring a lot of what would be considered "motivational" or "self-help" ideologies. By God's grace and through the confrontation of a brother, I saw my folly in this and was brought back from my wandering.

But the truth is that much of what I had learned from that sphere of thinking was actually true, as I have mentioned above. These people, although their motivations and goals were usually out of line with the Bible, nonetheless made many true observations about life. I wanted to share these things, but I was never fully comfortable embracing that purpose for my life because I didn't want to be guilty of simply helping people live a better life *now*—while they were on their way to hell. Remember, God never promises health, wealth, or prosperity in this life; and the Bible is quite clear that regardless of alleged earthly successes, *no one* enters heaven outside of a saving relationship with the Lord Jesus Christ (Matthew 7:21–23; Luke 9:25; John 3:3; 8:24; Acts 4:12).

I therefore caution you as you proceed. This is a dangerous book. The line that we're traversing here is a fine one, just as so many of the tensions we find in life and Scripture seem to be. We want to do well in this life, but we don't want to be like Demas, who, *in love with this present world*, abandoned the apostle Paul and the Christian faith (2 Timothy 4:10). My aim here is to help you live well and faithfully, but we must never confuse or confound that which is temporal with that which is eternal.

Michael Horton notes, "Our American gospel has become a gospel of following your dreams and being good so God will make all your dreams come true. But this has nothing to do with the God of the Bible." I want you to live wisely and well. I want your dreams to come true. But we live the way we live in light of who God is and what He has done, not to bend the will of God to accomplish our own desires. Thus, I have written this book to you, Christian, in the hope that you would do all that you do, whatever you do, and amid whatever may or may not come to pass, to His glory (1 Corinthians 10:31; Colossians 3:17).

The pages ahead represent some of the most important lessons that I've learned in my life—lessons that will generally present themselves to all of us at some point. We're going to talk about having a proper mindset, knowing yourself, and getting out of the infamous comfort zone. We're going to talk about rejection, about planning and taking action, and about perseverance. We're going to talk about disappointment and success. Lastly, we'll consider how all of this measures up when stacked against the reality of our mortality.

You'll face all these things in your own life, and your life will be a direct result of how you face them. That's a big deal! I want you to do well. I want you to be ready. I want you to respond faithfully. I want you to learn these lessons. I hope you'll be helped in all these areas by reading on, allowing your journey through this book to inform your journey through life.

> *Wisdom cries aloud in the street, in the markets she raises her voice; at the head of the noisy streets she cries out; at the entrance of the city gates she speaks: "How long, O simple ones, will you love being simple?" (Proverbs 1:20–22)*

This book is my exhortation to you—my crying out. Heed these words and these lessons. You have a real opportunity to faithfully maximize all that God has given you and will give you. Is youth really wasted on the young? Generally, it is; but it doesn't have to be that way. It doesn't have to be that way with you. So don't waste any more time. Begin today, begin now, seeking to do everything you do and to respond to everything that comes your way in the wisdom of our great God and Savior.

Journey well!

Your Kinsman and Servant,
Mick
January 2020
Youngstown, Ohio

CHAPTER 1:
Get in the Right Mindset

The soul becomes dyed with the color of its thoughts.
—Marcus Aurelius

You have to get in the right mindset. Your mindset in life is everything. You will not encounter a situation or scenario that will not be deeply affected by the mindset you have as you approach it. It was Henry Ford who said, "Whether you think you can, or think you can't—you're right." Ford is spot-on here, within reason of course. I may believe that I can fly, but if I jump off a building and flap my arms really quickly, it's not going to end well. So let's be reasonable here and save me from qualifying every single statement that follows.

We're talking about principles that, in general, are true. So Ford is right because what we ultimately do, as well as how we go about doing it, is a direct result of what we think. This is true in every sphere of life. Right belief begets right practice, and if you find yourself thinking wrongly about something, you're consequently going to behave or respond wrongly to that particular situation.

James Allen, in his classic work, *As a Man Thinketh*, notes that "The aphorism, 'as a man thinketh in his heart so is he,' not only embraces the whole of a man's being, but is so comprehensive as to reach out to every condition and circumstance of his life. A man is literally what he thinks, his character being the complete sum of all his thoughts."[5]

How true this is. Our thoughts govern us, often more than we realize, and consistent with Ford's observations, what we think has a way of manifesting itself in our actions and in our lives. Allen continues on this point: "A man's mind may be likened to a garden, which may be intelligently cultivated or allowed to run wild; but whether cultivated or neglected, it must, and will, bring forth. If no useful seeds are put into it, then an abundance of useless weed seeds will fall therein, and will continue to produce their kind."[6] So, then, we have to wonder what seeds we're allowing to take root in the garden of our mind. How diligent are we in cultivating our thoughts? By what standard do we plant and tend to them? The answers to these questions, even as Allen points out, will not only determine how we respond to things in life, but they'll form our character and become the compass directing the whole of our lives. Are you heading in the right direction? Is your compass properly fixated?

A Biblical Mindset

As you approach a myriad of situations, scenarios, trials, and opportunities in life, I encourage you to think properly about such things—to use *sober judgment* (Romans 12:3). Although this concept is universal and not only true of Christians, Christians uniquely have the mind of Christ (1 Corinthians 2:16). We have a special and (hopefully) biblical way of thinking about things. Even so, as we examine and seek to interpret the things around us, how do we know if we're interpreting them and thinking through

---

5   James Allen, *As a Man Thinketh* (New York: Jeremy P. Tarcher/Penguin, 2006), 3. First published 1902.

6   Allen, 11.

them properly? The answer is dependent upon what God has said about such things.

"What does the Bible say?" That is a question we don't often stop to ask, but in reality we would save ourselves a lot of hardship if we started there.

Perhaps my favorite framework in the Bible to demonstrate this principle is found in Psalm 73. There are so many things worth noting in this great psalm. Psalm 73 is about Asaph. More specifically, it's about Asaph's struggle, which he is quite open about, and how he came through that struggle. Let's take a look at what was going on and see what we can learn.

> *Truly God is good to Israel, to those who are pure in heart. (Psalm 73:1)*

The first thing to note here is that Asaph starts in a really good place. He has good theology and is thinking pretty well about things; after all, he did write part of the Bible. Asaph rightly recognizes the goodness of God. As we live our lives here as sojourners and aliens and deal with all the things that go along with living in a fallen world, the best counsel that can be given in any situation, particularly as we consider our mindset, is to go back to, reflect upon, and respond in accordance with what we know about the character of God. I constantly find myself going back to who I know God to be, and I try to let the reality of who He is inform my response to everything in life. That is what Asaph does here in his own struggle, and I believe God is herein giving us a model for how we are to think through and work through the various things we encounter in life.

Now while it is true that Asaph starts off in a very good place, a very good way of thinking, it only takes him a verse to fall away from that. Notice verses two and three below, and let Asaph's quick change in disposition be a warning to all of us that even if we are well taught, we are not beyond falling prey to such a plight. *Let anyone who thinks that he stands take heed lest he fall* (1 Corinthians 10:12).

> *But as for me, my feet had almost stumbled,*
>   *my steps had nearly slipped.*
> *For I was envious of the arrogant*
>   *when I saw the prosperity of the wicked.*
> *(Psalm 73:2–3)*

In just one verse, Asaph both recognizes and identifies his struggle for us. Such was his struggle that he had almost stumbled and nearly slipped. Why was he struggling like this? Because he was envying the prosperity of the wicked. I trust at one point or another you may have had the same kind of thoughts as Asaph had. In our prosperous and often decadent society, it's not hard to look at the possessions others have (that we don't) and to covet those things, to be envious of them. This was the plight of Asaph. In fact, he spends the bulk of this psalm telling us about all the things the wicked have that he doesn't. His comparison reaches its peak in verses 12–14:

> *Behold, these are the wicked;*
>   *always at ease, they increase in riches.*
> *All in vain have I kept my heart clean*
>   *and washed my hands in innocence.*
> *For all the day long I have been stricken*
>   *and rebuked every morning. (Psalm 73:12–14)*

Here Asaph quite intensely recognizes the stark contrast between his own life and the lives of those who don't know God. They are at ease and in riches, and he is stricken and rebuked. You can see how the very language he uses is meant to forcefully depict a very drastic antithesis.

What we really need to be mindful of here, though, is what is said in verse 13. Asaph takes a hard look at his efforts to live a life that is pleasing to God, and he basically concludes he isn't getting anything out of it. We need to be extremely careful of such a mindset. We don't live the lives we do because we think we're going to get something from God—do we? Such a mindset implies that we think we deserve something from God. In reality, we should be thankful that He doesn't choose to repay us according to our works (Psalm 103:10). Rather, we are to live our lives in a disposition of submissive gratitude for all that God has done for us. Our lives are the *result* of something God has already done for us, not the *cause* of some potential future blessing. Jesus said, *If you love me, you will keep my commandments* (John 14:15). We should be seeking after righteousness because of our love for God and because of what He has done for us, not bartering with God for the lusts of our hearts.

Trusting God through Disappointments

I used to work in public education. I had largely enjoyed the work I was doing and the people I worked with, so when a new position opened up in my building that would enable me to potentially be promoted into a more substantive role, I jumped on it.

I was fortunate enough to land an interview, and things seemed to be going pretty well. However, about fifteen minutes into it, the superintendent stopped me, told me that I wasn't a strong enough candidate, and cut the interview short. I was stunned. The possibility of that happening never even crossed my mind. I extracted a couple of lessons from this, but first I want to ask you: How would you have responded if you were in my shoes? Or better yet: How would you have *thought* about this situation? How you think about things—your *mindset*—the emphasis of this chapter, is indicative of the disposition of your heart and will greatly influence your character, your decisions, your responses, and your actions. It will greatly influence your entire life.

So put yourself in my shoes. People seem to think you do pretty good work, you have more direct experience in the building than any other external candidate, you're pretty well liked (at least you think so), and now is your chance for all your hard work to pay off and be recognized—and you don't even get a full interview. What are you thinking? Be honest with yourself here.

Now let me tell you the two lessons I took from this. First, hard work doesn't always pay off in this life, at least not in the way we think it will. As Christians, we're doing our work as unto the Lord and for His glory (Colossians 3:17, 23–24) and as such, our faithful work always pays off in the ultimate sense of things. The second lesson I learned from this is that just because your hard work doesn't appear to have paid off doesn't mean you've been wronged. Perhaps you're familiar with the reality that hard work doesn't always pay off, but when we think about this principle, we often think of it in a kind of self-righteous way that implies that we didn't get what we deserved or that we've been wronged in some way. This just isn't always the case.

God was very gracious to me in this situation, as He always is, but I want you to know about the mindset I had going into that interview. I was trusting God completely with whatever happened. I certainly cared about what happened. Trusting God doesn't necessitate apathy. I didn't apply for the job hoping that I wouldn't get it. My mind was made up, though. God was in control, and He was going to work this out however seemed best to Him, and I could trust that it would also be best for me. I wanted that job, but I held the desire loosely, allowing it to rest at the feet of our great God. When I walked away from that interview, I can honestly tell you that my day was not affected negatively in even the slightest way. That is the grace of God. That is the importance of having a biblical mindset.

Mindset has to do not only with how we view ourselves and others, but how we interpret the situations that come upon us in life. Disappointment when things don't work out is normal (more on this in subsequent chapters), and excitement or concern going into an important situation is normal, but falling into despair or panic when things don't work out betrays an ungodly mindset and the need to have our minds prayerfully renewed by the Word of God (Romans 12:2). My response, through the grace of God, was only possible because I had a proper view of the situation. God is in control and He knows what He's doing. It was such an encouragement to me to see my response here because I can tell you that even as recently as a month or so earlier, I wouldn't have responded so gracefully. Be encouraged, Christian, when you see God working these victories in your life, even if they seem small, for that is evidence that you are growing into His likeness.

I wasn't wronged in my situation. In fact, I really think the superintendent demonstrated good leadership toward me because he was upfront with me about where I stood as he sought the most qualified person for the position. He also told me to stop by his office (I was out of town and so we did a phone interview) and he would work with me to get me to where I needed to be for future opportunities. He was willing to invest in me. That is good leadership, and I respect him for that. The old me wouldn't have had that mindset. The old me would have been ready to punch a hole in the wall and succumb to the despair of not knowing what I was going to do now that this opportunity had not come to fruition.

The concept of mindset is related to all the other things we'll talk about in this book; that's why this chapter is first. No matter what we're talking about—disappointment, rejection, fear, success, how we view ourselves—mindset is going to be crucial in how we respond and live faithfully. As such, rest assured that the intricacies and implications of our mindset in different areas will be explored further in future chapters. In the instance of my job interview, it would have been easy for me to toss my hands up in the air and ask God if He knew what He was doing. It would have been easy for me to harbor bitterness, thinking I deserved something when I really didn't. It would have been easy for me to think I was being treated unjustly. Have you ever responded to life that way? That's what Asaph did in Psalm 73.

When things weren't going how he thought they should be going, he essentially threw his hands up in the air and asked, "What's the point of living for God? What am I getting out of this? *All in vain have I kept my heart clean*" (Psalm 73:13). Asaph has a serious problem here. But before we get on his case too much, we need to stop and ask ourselves how often we find ourselves with the same mindset. Are our motivations honoring to God, or are we trying to manipulate His will by our good works so we can get what we really want? Of course, we wouldn't come right out and say that, but the way we live often betrays that mindset. Such a disposition is extremely grievous to God as we find ourselves in a Romans 1 mindset, worshipping the gifts rather than the giver (Romans 1:25).

We have to be extremely careful of a mindset that leads us to conclude that things will go a certain way if we're faithful. That's what Asaph was doing. If we think rightly about such a disposition, though, I hope we see that this mindset is the height of arrogance. "Jesus Christ Himself was perfectly faithful, and yet He was persecuted, even by His friends. Do we think that we deserve better?"[7] Remember that no servant is greater than his master (John 13:16). We need to abandon the mindset of Asaph here. We need to rid ourselves of the mindset that says that if we just pray hard enough, or if we just do what God says, or if we go out of our way to share the gospel with someone, or if we go to church every Sunday, then God will surely give us what we're seeking.[8] God may indeed give you what you're seeking. He does entreat us to bring our requests before Him (Matthew 7:7–11; Luke 18:1), but His answer will be according to His good pleasure, not according to our alleged good works. The corollary of that is also true and is just as important. When things don't go as we would have hoped, when tragedy strikes, or when the grief is so real you can taste it, this doesn't necessarily mean that you're lacking in faith or you've done something wrong.

Thankfully, though, that is not the end of Asaph's plight. Although he finds himself in a bit of a funk, he doesn't remain there. We need to take a look at what he did to get out of that funk, and it all goes back to this whole idea of mindset, specifically a godly mindset that thinks God's thoughts after Him.

---

7   George Scipione, (lecture, Reformed Presbyterian Theological Seminary).

8   For a good treatment of this, see Sarah Walton, "*The Red Sea in Front of Me: Reaching for God in Despair*," Desiring God, October 19, 2017.

> *But when I thought how to understand this,*
> *it seemed to me a wearisome task,*
> *until I went into the sanctuary of God;*
> *then I discerned their end. (Psalm 73:16–17)*

In verse 16, Asaph tells us that he grew weary in trying to understand the way things were playing out around him. Why would God allow the wicked to prosper in such a way while he was so stricken? Have you ever had something happen (or not happen) to you that you just didn't understand? This verse teaches us that we're not always going to understand the reason things are the way they are. I've had countless situations in my life that haven't gone how I would have liked them to. For example, I'm still not exactly sure why I didn't get that job. Sometimes things that seem like such good things just don't work out. We don't always understand why, but we can persevere through such disappointments, subservient to God's grace, by having a proper mindset, by interpreting the situation as God would have us interpret it, and ultimately by trusting in His goodness. Nonetheless, it often proves to be a wearisome task.

Such is the case with Asaph, but he does come up with some answers as he begins to think properly about his situation. In verse 17, he really begins to understand why things are the way they are and how wrong he's been in his thinking. Verse 17 serves as the hinge of this entire psalm; it's the turning point, and it's demonstrative of Asaph beginning to think properly and righteously about what he had previously been observing and interpreting very poorly. In his case, he undoubtedly went into an actual sanctuary, but for us, we might consider this as a directive to go back to God. We need to look at things through the lens of Scripture. When Asaph began to do this, his attitude and response to his situation drastically changed.

Asaph changed his mindset. He adjusted his worldview—or perhaps he was simply deliberate in actually applying the worldview he claimed to hold. As we consider counseling ourselves through such trials and hardships, concepts of mindset and worldview become particularly important. "If you would just adopt [a biblical understanding] of your problem, then your problem would either go away or get better or at least make sense."[9]

In Asaph's case, he adjusted his view and began to see the way things really were; he discerned the end of the wicked. He began to see that their prosperity, what initially appeared to be a great blessing, was truly a slippery place. He began to understand that God giving them such ease was actually God's judgment upon them. For only when we find ourselves at our end do we see our need for God and reach out for Him. People living in such ease will likely never know such want, and consequently will likely never see their great need for God. Sometimes we think God is keeping us from great blessings, when in reality He is keeping us from a slippery path. He knows what's best for us; we often don't—even though we like to think we do.

This passage is in no way teaching that there's something inherently wrong or sinful about wealth. But again, as a general rule, the Bible juxtaposes those people prospering in the world and living a life of ease with the people of God, who often find themselves persecuted, stricken, or suffering (Psalm 34:19; 2 Timothy 3:12). At the same time, God is pleased to bless His people with good gifts to be enjoyed with thanksgiving (1 Timothy 4:4–5). We do not need to walk around wishing to be miserable or to undergo some trial (Colossians 2:23). The point is that when such trials do come (and they will—see John 16:33), we who trust in Christ will be enabled to persevere by our faith, will be sanctified through that process, and will be assured of our salvation by our faithful response (1 Peter 1:6–7).

In the remaining verses, those subsequent to Asaph's change in mindset, we see Asaph recognize the truth of his situation and that of the wicked (verses 18–20), repent (verses 21–22), recognize the wisdom and truth that God's Word provides for him (verse 24), and reaffirm a right view of God (verses 25–26):

---

9   Heath Lambert, "Sufficiency of Scripture."

Whom have I in heaven but you?
  And there is nothing on earth that I desire
  besides you.
My flesh and my heart may fail,
  But God is the strength of my heart
  and my portion forever. (Psalm 73:25–26)

We see Asaph finish in the same place he started—with a right way of thinking. Again, this acts as a sobering warning to all of us. Even those of us who attend sound churches and sit under faithful teaching, even those who read their Bibles and pray regularly, are not beyond falling into sin and are not beyond falling prey to an improper mindset. The warning of Hebrews 2:1 rings true as we consider this reality: *Therefore we must pay much closer attention to what we have heard, lest we drift away from it.*

If this can happen to Asaph, it can certainly happen to us. We need to be all the more diligent to ensure that we're staying close to the truths God has given us in His Word and that we're living in the light of them. It will be to our benefit, both temporally and eternally, and God will thereby be glorified.

Importance of Biblical Thinking

So what's the big-picture takeaway from all of this? First off, although I hope we come away from this chapter with a sense of how important biblical thinking is, I need to mention that the Christian life is not simply about thinking properly. It also involves engaging the living God and having a deep and growing relationship with Him.

With that in mind, the lesson here is that we need to make sure we have a proper mindset as we live our lives. We need to allow such a mindset to steer us in the right direction. We need to appropriately value the various aspects of life and eternity. We need to think about ourselves, about God, and about the events that are happening both around us and to us. Having a proper mindset is how Asaph persevered through his own struggle, and it's how we'll persevere through the struggles that will inevitably come our way, or that even may be currently befalling us.

Note, too, that we aren't talking here about some Peter Pan strategy that simply says, "Think happy thoughts," and everything will magically be better. Rather, we need to prayerfully recognize our need for God's grace in all that we do, including how we see and interpret the things around us. We need to think God's thoughts after Him. We need to always look at the world through Bible-tinted glasses lest we find ourselves in a toilsome way. Remember, becoming a Christian doesn't mean that things are going to always be perfect. In fact, Jesus tells us it will be the opposite (John 16:33), but by the way of His grace and the means of His Word, He has richly provided for us all that we need to persevere to the end.

Journey well.

CHAPTER 2:
Know Yourself

The unexamined life is not worth living.
—Socrates

You have to know yourself. So many people today, to their detriment, go through life with very little self-awareness. Augustine observed that "Men go abroad to admire the heights of mountains, the mighty waves of the sea, the broad tides of rivers, the compass of the ocean, and the circuits of the stars, and pass themselves by [without a thought]."[10] Doesn't it seem odd that we go to such great lengths to know things that are outside of us or are far away from us, but put forth so little effort in actually coming to a realization of who we are, what we want, and who God has made us to be? While it is, of course, true that you come to a greater understanding of who you are as you live your life and go through various experiences, self-reflection is also important.

---

10   Saint Augustine, *The Confessions of Saint Augustine*, trans. Edward B. Pusey (Digireads, 2015), 265.

For one thing, going through life will afford you very little if you don't spend sufficient time assimilating the lessons you've learned and the impact they've had on your character. Without this reflection, we generally end up making the same mistakes over and over again due to our tendencies, and without being aware of the error in those tendencies, we're prone to keep them close. We really don't know what we don't know, and that's why ignorance is so dangerous and the pursuit of wisdom is so important.

I can tell you personally that coming to know who I am before God and others has been, among other things, a great source of confidence. Sometimes we let what others think of us have far too large an impact on our actions. The truth is that we have to live in such a way as to not let the thoughts of others govern our own lives. While we're not the captain of our life (God is), we *are* the first mate; and the last time I checked, the first mate considers what others say, but when the captain lets him take control of the helm, he steers the ship in the direction he believes is best. This is how we need to live our lives. We cannot allow ourselves to become prisoners of the thoughts of others.

Considering the Counsel of Others

Yes, we can listen to the thoughts of others without being prisoner to them. My good friend Jeff is a great example of this. He's been a lot of help to me as I came to realize much of what's in this book. God has been gracious in providing many mentors in my life, and I encourage you to find one (or as many as you can). You have to reach out to people, though. Many are willing to help, but they aren't mind readers.

Jeff is a really interesting guy. When he was in high school, he was in a horrible accident that left him scarred for life. He lost half of both his hands and one of his eyes. It appeared he would be quite limited in what he could accomplish. One day his high school guidance counselor came up to him and told him that he found a way for Jeff to get help going to college. Because of Jeff's "disability," he would basically be able to go to any university in the country for free. What a great opportunity! Most people would seize something like this without a moment's consideration—not Jeff, though.

Jeff declined and decided not to go to college. His guidance counselor thought he was foolish, and I'm sure just about everyone else did too. Today, though, Jeff is one of the most successful people I know. He ended up going into business for himself. He was a nationally recognized insurance salesman, had countless profitable real estate enterprises, and now spends his days basically doing whatever he wants. Don't think that means sipping piña coladas and taking it easy somewhere, though. Jeff is also one of the hardest working people I know. When he's not reconstructing houses and building stone pizza ovens from scratch, he's pouring into his family and younger guys like me.

My point is this: if Jeff had allowed the thoughts of everyone else to govern his decisions, he would not be where he is today. If he had taken advantage of the scholarship and gone to college, I am sure that he would have done fine, but he would have been doing something that he ultimately knew wasn't right for him. This is where we have to be discerning in taking the counsel of others (more on this in chapter 6). Most of the decisions you make in life are not going to be between something good and something bad. Those are always easy decisions. Most of the decisions you make are going to be between what's good and what's best. In this case, and again in most of the cases you encounter in your own life, you aren't (I hope) going to be deciding on whether or not you should do something that is sinful.

Jeff could have honored God by going to college. But he also honored God by going the route he did, provided his motivations were good, and I trust they were. Sometimes, in instances such as these, you have to do what's right for you. Remember, you may not be the captain of your life, but you're the one whom God entrusted with it. For many, probably most of us, taking that scholarship would have been the way to go—but it wasn't for Jeff. This is why it is important to know yourself. There's not much worse than being somewhere you know you shouldn't be and doing something you know you shouldn't be doing. The only way to know those things is to know yourself.

Know Your Gifts and Talents

In knowing yourself, you should also have an awareness—a self-awareness—of the gifts and interests that you've been given by God. Often gifts and interests go hand in glove. I don't know too many people who enjoy doing things they're not good at, although sometimes we have to put in some work to become proficient in things. Actually, I would say that's true of all things, even something you're particularly gifted in. Think about the people who are the best at what they do, whatever that might be. They have talent to be sure, but I can assure you they also put in the hard work to develop that talent. It's been said that hard work trumps talent, so whatever conclusions you come to here, make sure you put in the time and the work.

What do you enjoy doing? What are you good at? What gifts do you have that you could enjoy developing? A good biblical anthropology recognizes that our hearts are deceitfully wicked (Jeremiah 17:9), but we need to be careful of putting many of the good desires God gives us in that category. If you have a particular interest in music, medicine, writing, or teaching, you need to understand that those particular interests are likely from God. I look at some of the things some people enjoy doing, and I know I could never do them. They don't interest me, but clearly they interest others. So take a self-inventory of your gifts and interests.

You'll find—and you'll see this more and more as you get older—that you don't really know everything about yourself. As we've already mentioned, you find out many of these things as you go through the journey of life. For example, I never seriously considered being anything other than a teacher. It seemed like a clear path for me, and I never second-guessed that path (at least not until many years later). Even though I may not currently be a teacher in the traditional sense, I can look back and see that God used all that experience to develop the gifts He had given me—gifts that I didn't even really know I had at the time. God has given me communication gifts. I love speaking and teaching and preaching. I never feel more alive than when I'm doing those things; but let me tell you that it wasn't always that way, even when I was a professional teacher.

I remember my first experience having my very own classroom and being up front teaching. I thought I was doing great until one of the freshman girls raised her hand and asked me if I was scared to be up there. I was like, "Huh?" She said, "Yeah, you're not looking at any of us when you're up there teaching." Sure enough, she was right. I was just kind of staring off into the distance, pretending to be looking at all of them without actually looking at anyone. Over the years, though, God put me in situations where that gift could be developed.

I was teaching at my job, I was teaching at church, and I was even filling pulpits in other local churches. Now, after looking back and taking a self-inventory, I realize I want to be using what God has given me, and I want to spend my life doing it as long as He permits. If you're following along with me but still not sure what that looks like for you, don't fret. I'm still not exactly sure what it looks like for me, either, but I'm trusting that writing this book is a step in the right direction.

A Biblical Look at Self-Esteem

As I mentioned in the introduction, this book walks the line that borders biblical truth and unbiblical ideology. As such, particularly in this context, we need to consider the sentiments of self-esteem and self-confidence. These ideas tend to be quite pervasive, especially when looking at what is coming out of the self-help/ motivational genre. Such sentiments are generally not biblical though. As Christians, we should never be looking inward for our strength to accomplish things here in this world. Our strength to accomplish anything and everything comes from above (Psalm 28:7). It comes from God, and we can do nothing apart from Him (John 15:5). We move forward in any endeavor in life only insofar as He allows us (James 4:15). This means, too, that the whole concept of self-esteem and our need for it just isn't biblical.

But haven't you ever gone into a situation giving yourself a pep talk, saying something like, "I've got this!"? Perhaps you've walked in to take a final exam you spent the whole week studying for saying, "I've got this!" Perhaps you've arrived at a job interview saying, "I've got this!" Perhaps you finally asked that special someone out for coffee thinking, *I've got this—and I don't even really like coffee!* Is that the same thing as self-esteem? Is it wrong thinking to say that to yourself in any myriad of situations you might be approaching?

Well, not necessarily, but it could be. We need to consider a couple of ideas here. The first is that there's nothing wrong with such a mindset or statement or pep talk, as long as we recognize that "We got this" only because God allows us to. Remember, there are a whole lot of things we have to get up and do in this life and there are a whole lot of times when we need to take action—but the Christian life is not about pulling yourself up by your bootstraps and getting after it. Rather, it's about recognizing that we don't even have bootstraps outside of the grace of God, and *He* is the one who enables us to do anything. You need to recognize that, thank Him for that, and ask for His continued help (Psalm 105:4)—and *then, and only then,* do "You got this!" We aren't always good at recognizing this foundational truth in the moment, but we should really get better at it.

If what we're saying is true about recognizing God's provision, though, is there really any room for saying "I've got this"? Don't such considerations look to ourselves and not to Him? Don't they get pretty close to self-confidence and self-esteem? Good questions, but with subservience to recognizing that God enables us to do such things and gives us all the good things we have, such real and practical assessments of ourselves are not only appropriate, but they're also wise and even commanded in Scripture.

For by the grace given to me I say to everyone among you not to think of himself more highly than he ought to think, but to think with sober judgment, each according to the measure of faith that God has assigned. (Romans 12:3)

So as you can see, there is a place for an honest and sober assessment of what you possess. Paul tells us to make a *sober judgment*. It is not arrogant or proud to recognize that you've been given certain gifts or abilities, or even to have confidence in something because you've trained and prepared for it; rather, it is commanded. Some people are prone to think that saying you excel at something or that you're good at something necessitates a lack of humility, but such is not the case. In fact, to ignore or downplay one's talents is the real demonstration of pride. False humility is pride. All of us have been given certain gifts. We have been given different gifts, to different degrees, to be used in different contexts and in different ways. It is incumbent upon us to be accurate in our self-assessment so we can best put to use what God has seen fit to give us.

It's also interesting to note that Paul warns us in this passage about thinking too highly of ourselves. If the self-esteem gurus have it right, such a warning wouldn't make sense. The proponents of this type of thinking generally advocate that your lack of self-esteem is the problem and that you couldn't possibly think too highly of yourself. Scripture assumes the opposite though. Scripture knows our tendencies and our hearts, and it assumes (correctly) that our opinion of ourselves is generally too high. Paul gives a similar warning in Galatians 6:3: *If anyone thinks he is something, when he is nothing, he deceives himself.* Clearly, our problem isn't low self-esteem; it's pride. Jay Adams notes:

Many people who are accepting the self-esteem teachings not only "deceive" themselves by thinking that they are something when they are nothing (that's bad enough), but they exult over it and teach God's little ones to do the same. It is to keep people from exulting over how good they are that Paul wrote these words. [Furthermore,] a sober evaluation is made not on the basis of how well one is doing in comparison with others, but by comparing one's work with scriptural standards.[11]

Adams emphasizes the importance of having the right mindset regarding ourselves. So to bring our discussion somewhat full circle in terms of our reflection at the beginning of this chapter, in the same way that we can't let the thoughts of others govern our lives, we must also beware of comparing ourselves to others (2 Corinthians 10:12). I have yet to think of an example in which this is helpful, and Adams notes above that such a comparison is not part of any sober evaluation. We are to examine our own work here (Galatians 6:4), and not the work of others.

The Dangers of an Entitled Mindset

Akin to the self-esteem ideology, there are a lot of mantras out there that try to motivate people to go out and "get what they deserve." Be careful of that kind of mindset. If we're thinking properly, if we're thinking biblically, we actually deserve hell (Romans 6:23). We are born into this world as children of wrath (Ephesians 2:3), and we deserve none of the good things that God has given us (Romans 11:35). We need to understand that we don't actually deserve anything, at least not anything good. So moving toward a place of success or praying and moving toward a particular endeavor isn't about getting what you deserve; rather, it's about glorifying God. This is completely antithetical to what is being trumpeted in our society today.

---

11   Jay Adams, *The Biblical View of Self-Esteem, Self-Love, & Self Image* (Eugene, OR: Harvest House, 1986), 117–118.

The pampering of the modern mind has resulted in a population that feels deserving of something without earning that something, a population that feels they have a right to something without sacrificing for it. People declare themselves experts, entrepreneurs, inventors, innovators, mavericks, and coaches without any real-life experience. And they do this not because they actually think they are greater than everybody else; they do it because they feel they need to be great to be accepted in a world that broadcasts only the extraordinary.[12]

There are a few things we should say about this powerful observation by author Mark Manson. The first is simply that when we talk about "earning" something, we're talking about the general economy of how the world works, and not about salvation, which is always by grace (Ephesians 2:8–9). The second is that we really do live in a world that only broadcasts the extraordinary. Even among Christians, very little concern is generally given for the scriptural exhortations to live a quiet and simple life (1 Thessalonians 4:11; 1 Timothy 2:2). After all, that seems pretty mediocre, and who wants that? We will reflect a bit more on this in the chapter about success, but suffice it now to simply ask, "Are we really willing to take things that God commends and call them *mediocre*?"

The last thing to note here is that we also really do live in a society that has embraced a mentality of entitlement at all levels. We sometimes have a tendency to think that we're owed something, either by others or by society itself, and nothing could be further from the truth. We briefly touched on the ultimate sense of this principle—that ultimately we deserve the just wrath of God for our sins. That is why we need the mercy, forgiveness, and grace of God that is found only in the cross of Christ (Romans 5:8; 2 Corinthians 5:21).

---

12   Mark Manson, *The Subtle Art... : A Counterintuitive Approach to Living a Good Life* (New York: Harper Collins, 2016), 207.

We deserve hell. It doesn't get any worse than that. What I want you to see, though, is that if we're thinking rightly about this, then that principle necessarily informs anything lesser that we think we might be owed. Notwithstanding the economy of things in this world (i.e., I go to work and earn a paycheck that I am, of course, *owed*; and we see this axiom demonstrated in a myriad of different contexts), we're really not owed anything.

Let me give you an example from my own life. As I mention several times throughout this book, I have applied for and have been rejected for many job opportunities. Remember my interview in chapter one? A similar situation arose when I became aware of a student pastor position at a local church in my hometown. My church has a fairly good relationship with that church, and I'm even friends with some of the pastors on staff there, so I reached out to them. They were very gracious and agreed to meet up for lunch to discuss why I thought I'd be a good fit for the position and to inform me of some of the dynamics of the situation. In the end, I wasn't even called for an interview. I found myself pretty upset about this. *My friends were pastors there! Didn't they care that I wanted this job? They should do something for me! I should have this position!* And then, by God's grace, it eventually hit me how stupid that line of thinking was.

Is that how friendship works? Do we believe that our friends owe us something simply because they're our friends? What high opinions of ourselves must we have if that's how we think! Surely Paul's words to the Galatians that we considered come to mind here (Galatians 6:3).

My friends didn't owe me anything. In fact, they already went out of their way to have lunch with me. The fault in me not getting the job, or even an interview, was not theirs. If it was anyone's, it was my own. I either didn't have the necessary qualifications or I did an inadequate job of demonstrating that I did. Or, akin to my situation in chapter one, no one was at fault—it just wasn't meant to be. One thing is clear, though: no one owed me anything in that situation, and generally no one owes us anything in life. Remember that.

Coming to a Greater Self-Awareness

As you move forward in life and are informed by the many experiences you'll have, you'll also be guided in some measure by the
self-awareness we keep mentioning. You're going to come to a better
understanding of what you want your life to look like. You'll have
more-informed answers to life's questions: Where do you want
to be? What do you want to be? Who do you want to be? If you
follow the principles in this book, you'll have some good ideas
about how to answer those questions, and it'll be a great help to
you in recognizing opportunities and making decisions. Without
self-awareness, though, you'll largely be lost and without direction.

It's okay, too, if your answers to life's questions change. In fact,
I'll tell you now that they *are* going to change. Some will see them
change in small ways and some will see them change in big ways,
but they will definitely change. Even if such changes cause you
to do an about-face and take your life in a completely different
direction, don't be discouraged; it's part of the journey. Any plans
we make for our lives are our servants, not our masters. It's good
to have them and follow them, but God always has the right to
interrupt them,[13] and generally speaking, we have the right to
change them as we see fit.

There is one last thing as we consider this very important aspect
of knowing yourself, and that is the very real presence of very
real emotions in everything we experience in this life. Emotions
are a gift from God, but they're strong, and we often let them
master us. Make sure that you're a slave to Christ and a slave
to righteousness rather than a slave to your emotions (Romans
6:16–17). Your emotions are going to tell you to do all kinds of
things that God would have you stay clear from, and they will
lead you to decisions and conclusions that aren't necessarily best,

---

13   Joe Propri, *Parenting Put Simply: Biblical Instruction for Raising Kids,*
#106 (Biblical Counseling Institute, 2008), DVD.

right, or true. You might even wrongly perceive your emotions to be leadings of some sort from God Himself.

Emotions often cloud our judgment. Emotions might tempt us to marry a non-believer, break our commitments, go after all the shiny things of the world, stay in bed on Sunday morning, or seek to divorce our spouse under the pretense of not being in love anymore—all because we either *felt* like doing something or didn't *feel* like doing something. That's not how we are supposed to live, though. We need to do what we *know* to be right, not what we *feel* to be right. They aren't always the same thing. John Piper writes this about emotions as we consider them in this context:

> *My feelings are not God. God is God. My feelings do not define truth. God's Word defines truth. My feelings are echoes and responses to what my mind perceives. And sometimes—many times—my feelings are out of sync with the truth. When that happens—and it happens every day in some measure—I try not to bend the truth to justify my imperfect feelings, but rather, I plead with God: Purify my perceptions of your truth and transform my feelings so that they are in sync with the truth.*[14]

As you continue on your journey of life, you're going to learn many things about yourself. You're going to realize one day, as you look back on who you were, that you're not even close to the same person. We change and we grow every day. Self-awareness is very important in all of this. It will help you acknowledge your tendencies and master your feelings. It will help you look at your life and apply the lessons you've learned. It will help you recognize and cultivate your gifts and your desires.

As you come to know yourself, you will gain better discernment regarding which decisions in life make sense and which ones

---

14   John Piper, *Finally Alive* (Fearn, Scotland: Christian Focus, 2009), 165.

don't. You'll have a better understanding of how you can serve and glorify God with what He's given you. Ultimately, though, you can only truly come to know yourself insofar as you know yourself in relationship to God.

This means not only recognizing our sinful tendencies and condemnation outside of Christ (John 3:36), but it also means living in light of who you are in Him. You are a new creature (2 Corinthians 5:17) with the power of the Holy Spirit dwelling inside you (Romans 8:9; 2 Timothy 1:7). You are a son or daughter of God, a child of God (Galatians 4:7), living in light of the resurrection of Jesus Christ (Romans 6:5) and walking here as one who is seated with Him in the heavenly places (Ephesians 2:6). You have been forgiven (Isaiah 1:18), and there's no condemnation for those who are in Christ Jesus (Romans 8:1). Christ is your life (Colossians 3:4)!

Isn't that incredible? Above all else that you work through in the area of knowing yourself, this is who you are. Constantly keep that before you, and live in light of this glorious truth. Therein lies all the confidence and hope you'll ever need.

Journey well.

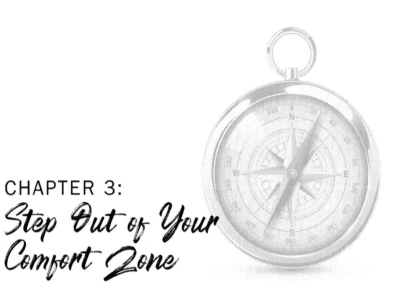

CHAPTER 3:
Step Out of Your Comfort Zone

If you don't go after what you want, you'll never have
it. If you don't ask, the answer is always no. If you
don't step forward, you're always in the same place.
—NORA ROBERTS

*Y*ou have to step out of your comfort zone. Despite its apparent safety, it's an extremely dangerous place. Every default action we take is undergirded with the idea and presupposition that we must preserve our lives. This fight for preservation can be seen in everything we do and in all of our natural tendencies. "We are not designed to do things that are uncomfortable or scary or difficult. Our brains are designed to protect us from those things because our brains are trying to keep us alive."[15] So when we perceive that something will be difficult or uncomfortable, we

---

15   Mel Robbins, *"Mel Robbins on Why Motivation Is Garbage,"* https://www.youtube.com/watch?v=X54GQFS_ouM.

hesitate and we start to feel nervous, worried, anxious, and fearful. That's our brains saying, "Don't do that! Stay safe!"

Most of us, therefore, spend our lives seeking safety, only to come to the end of our journey and realize that despite all our seeking, we never actually reached that safety. Earl Nightingale observes, "Most people tiptoe their way through life, hoping they make it safely to death." The truth, though, is that we all inevitably die, and for the illusion of safety, we have paid the ultimate price—our lives. Every time you run in the other direction in the face of adversity, or when you take the easy way out or give in to this self-preservation and retreat to the infamous comfort zone, you give up an opportunity to live your life. It could be said that in trying to save your life, you lose it. Didn't Jesus say something like that (Luke 9:24)?

For a long time, if you had asked me what I wanted to do with my life, I would have answered that I wanted to teach at a university. Then this idea got a little bit refined, and I would have said that I would really like to teach theology at a university. Then I put legs to this idea and started looking into what I needed to do and where I needed to go. A lot of us get this far in a lot of our endeavors, but there are two remaining components: the means whereby we can actually execute an endeavor, and the execution itself. We might also add commitment in there.

Years ago now, a very gracious friend offered to pay my way to go to seminary. He handed me a check for $10,000 and said, "Go." What astounding generosity! What gracious provision from God! You might expect me to tell you that I took that check and went away to finish my master's degree. After all, who could pass up such an opportunity?

Well, remember, we are talking about comfort zones in this chapter, and I'm sorry to say I chickened out. Sometime later, after some more planning and a visit to the seminary in Louisville, Kentucky, I ended up handing him back his check. He was noticeably surprised, as I recall. I think at some point I'd like to ask him more specifically what he was thinking. I trust he was trying to figure out what on earth I was thinking.

Plain and simple: I chickened out. I couldn't leave my comfort zone. I clearly wasn't committed to doing what was necessary to achieve my goal. You have to have that commitment, too, because your brain is always going to kick in. Those distress signals and warning signals are always going to say, "Stay safe," and only the truly committed are resolved enough to move forward.

I passed up an incredible opportunity because of fear and lack of commitment, embracing instead a desire for safety and an unwillingness to make sacrifices. All this was not demonstrative of the fact that I didn't want to go (I really did), but that I wanted everything I had more; but what did I actually have? I had nothing except my comfort zone that was, little by little, chloroforming me to a life of failure.

When was the last time someone instantaneously provided you with the means you needed to make your dreams come true? Has anyone ever handed you a $10,000 check just because they believed in you and wanted to see you do well? Such opportunities are the things of fairy tales.

It's Worth the Pursuit

There is certainly a treacherous pursuit involved in seeking to leave your comfort zone, but by the very nature of it, what lies on the other side is always worth that pursuit. Even if you take one step outside your comfort zone and you fall flat on your face, you learn, you grow, and you build resilience. The next step out is a little bit easier and a little bit farther, until fall after fall you nonetheless look back and say, "I may have been on the ground so much that I'm covered in dirt, but look how far I've come." It's not always about the results. You have to learn to love the process. Living is a lot more about the journey than the destination. Yes, it's cliché, but clichés are clichés for a reason.

I'm not really too much into sports, and consequently I'm not really into films about sports, but one of the great movies of my time is *Rudy*. If you haven't seen this film, perhaps you should put the book down for a bit and take care of that. I commend it wholeheartedly to you. It is the story of Notre Dame football player Rudy Ruettiger, who chased hard after his dream to play football for the University of Notre Dame. In what I trust was a fairly accurate depiction, Sean Astin, better known as Samwise Gamgee, portrayed the tenacious Rudy, who is only 5'7"—not exactly the poster child for competitive college football. There's a scene in that film, though, that strikes at the heart of the point we're making here. Rudy walks into a church to pray, and a priest who is very familiar with his situation comes up to him and engages him in conversation:

> *Priest: [in church] Taking your appeal to a higher authority?*
> *Rudy: I'm desperate. If I don't get in next semester, it's over. Notre Dame doesn't accept senior transfers.*
> *Priest: Well, you've done a hell of a job kid, chasing down your dream.*
> *Rudy: Who cares what kind of job I did if it doesn't produce results? It doesn't mean anything.*
> *Priest: I think you'll find that it will.*[16]

"I think you'll find that it will." I would submit the same to you. Even if you don't achieve all that you set out to, even if you're rejected and ridiculed (which Rudy was), such experiences will build your character and turn you into the person you're supposed to be. I can tell you that from experience. "Adversity builds character."[17] The apostle Paul alludes to the same thing: *Not only that, but we rejoice in our sufferings, knowing that suffering produces endurance, and endurance produces character, and character produces hope* (Romans 5:3–4).

---

16   https://www.imdb.com/title/tt0108002/characters/nm0000276

17   Ken Sande, *The Peacemaker: A Biblical Guide to Resolving Personal Conflict*, 3rd ed. (Grand Rapids: Baker Books, 2004), 37.

The apostle Paul was well acquainted with adversity (2 Corinthians 11:16–33; 2 Timothy 4:6). He went ahead on his journey to accomplish what he knew he had to do, knowing full well that suffering awaited him. To be more specific, *imprisonment and afflictions* awaited him (Acts 20:23). Perhaps Paul's context was a little different than your own, as he was charged with such a particular and monumental ministry from the Lord Himself, whom he personally saw (Acts 9:3–6), but this axiom nonetheless held true for Paul. He certainly wasn't constrained by his comfort zone, unless you think that imprisonment and affliction were somehow comfortable for him. Remember, he may have been the apostle Paul, but he was human just like you and me, and he had the same Spirit of God dwelling in him, empowering him to move forward (Colossians 1:29).

Fear Akin to Laziness

Living within your comfort zone, always seeking safety, and always taking the path of least resistance isn't going to afford you much in this life. More than that, I would submit to you that such a disposition and way of living is really dishonoring to the Lord. Jesus tells a parable that teaches as much. The parable is found in Matthew 25:14–30, the parable of the talents.[18] The parable is about a wealthy businessman who goes on a long trip, but before he leaves, he entrusts three of his servants with a certain amount of money or "talents," which in this context is a form of currency.

> *For it will be like a man going on a journey, who called his servants and entrusted to them his property.*

---

18 The majority of my studying and, thus, information concerning a biblical understanding of this passage as it is used throughout this book was primarily taken from sermons from Brian Borgman, John MacArthur, and Tim Conway on the same passage. Additional reference was given to the *New Testament Commentary: Matthew* by William Hendriksen.

> *To one he gave five talents, to another two, to another one, to each according to his ability. Then he went away. He who had received the five talents went at once and traded with them, and he made five talents more. So also he who had the two talents made two talents more. But he who had received the one talent went and dug in the ground and hid his master's money. (Matthew 25:14–18)*

We're talking about an extraordinary amount of money here. On the low end, even the servant who was given only one talent was likely entrusted with the better part of a million dollars. The servants were given stewardship of what belonged to their master, and it was thus incumbent upon them to dutifully work to bring the master a return on his investment. We see that two of the servants did just that, but one of the servants went and hid what was given to him in the ground. When we stay in our comfort zones and fail to step out in faith, we're essentially taking what God has given us and burying it in the ground. Now I'm not talking about doing crazy and unwise things. God is a God of order, and He would have us live in a wise way, but I am talking about avoiding a life that is crippled by fear, laziness, or both. Fear and laziness are very closely related to each other, especially in the context of considering our comfort zones. What things in your life are you burying?

At some point in Jesus's story, the master returned and settled accounts with his servants. This was their day of reckoning. To the servants who had acted upon what the master had given them, a commendation was in order. The servants had acted wisely. They had done what was required of them, they had made use of what was given to them, and they were rewarded for it. But things did not go so well for the servant who took what the master had given him and buried it in the ground:

> *He also who had received the one talent came forward, saying, "Master, I knew you to be a hard man,*

> *reaping where you did not sow, and gathering where you scattered no seed, so I was afraid, and I went and hid your talent in the ground. Here, you have what is yours." But his master answered him, "You wicked and slothful servant! You knew that I reap where I have not sown and gather where I scattered no seed? Then you ought to have invested my money with the bankers, and at my coming I should have received what was my own with interest. So take the talent from him and give it to him who has the ten talents." (Matthew 25:24–28)*

We might have been tempted to shrug off this servant's behavior, but the master, representative of Christ in this parable, was not happy at all. He said to him, *You wicked and slothful servant!* The servant had described his master as a hard man and had used this as an excuse to bury what he had been given. This was evidence that he didn't actually know his master at all. Our God is not a *hard* God; He is merciful, loving, and compassionate (Psalm 86:15). However, as if to go along with his servant's argument, the master tells him that he didn't even do the bare minimum. He didn't even take what he was given and give it to the bankers. This was unacceptable in the sight of the master.

The wicked servant said that he was afraid, but the master called him slothful. Notice how the Bible recognizes the relationship between fear and laziness here, as well as in the book of Proverbs: *The sluggard says, "There is a lion outside! I shall be killed in the streets!"* (Proverbs 22:13).

In this passage in Proverbs, the sluggard, the lazy person, claims that there is a lion in the streets so he can't leave his house to go work. He is seeking safety, and under the pretense of a legitimate threat, just like in the parable, he aims to justify his laziness.

"Biblically, laziness is an ethical issue."[19] We need to beware of it. Fearing to step outside of our comfort zones can be a form of laziness, for in such moments we are idolizing our comfort and avoiding difficulty at all costs. We fail to do what we know we should. This is laziness. What allegedly legitimate threats are you using to justify your inaction? What lions are in the streets of your life?

Actor Will Smith tells of his experience stepping out of an airplane to skydive. He talks about the crippling fear that grips the heart as one is ready to jump from the plane. He describes the experience: standing at the edge of the plane, ready to jump out, listening to the instructor counting down—1... 2... and then being pushed out of the plane on "2" because on "3" everyone grabs the side of the plane and holds on for dear life. Smith then describes the sensation of going from crippling fear to indescribable bliss in an instant, simply being free and gliding through the air.[20] Now I've never been skydiving, but what a great illustration. Smith concludes that "God placed the best things in life on the other side of terror," on the other side of that imaginary line of safety, just outside of the comfort zone.

I've lived most of my life within the comfort zone—paralyzed, timid, and afraid to do what should be done. Mind you, there's nothing directly stated in the Bible commanding me to go away to seminary, but aside from just being plain stupid, I believe that succumbing to fear in this situation was sinning against God. I didn't trust Him. I clung to comfort and familiarity. I was lazy, unwilling to seize the opportunity that He had given me, an opportunity for which I had been praying earnestly. I would implore you not to live a life characterized by such fear. You never know what you're going to be passing up.

---

19   Brian Borgman, "The Parable of the Talents" (sermon, Minden, NV, June 4, 2003).

20   Will Smith, *Facing Your Fears*, https://www.youtube.com/watch?v=MHnYpcmc2m0.

Remember, God gave us a spirit, not of fear or of timidity, but of power (2 Timothy 1:7). You have to step out, take action, and go for it, whether that's going away to college, applying for a job, going on a mission trip, asking that girl out for coffee, or just going on a random adventure. Do it, and do it now! John A. Shedd observed that "A ship in harbor is safe, but that is not what ships are built for." Think about that and get on out to sea.

Journey well.

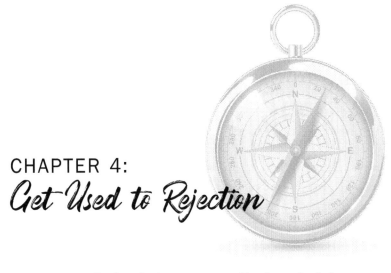

CHAPTER 4:
Get Used to Rejection

*I take rejection as someone blowing a bugle in my ear
to wake me up and get going, rather than retreat.*
—SYLVESTER STALLONE

*Y*ou have to get used to rejection. Rejection is part of life. It doesn't matter who you are or what you do—it's going to happen. Rejection is no respecter of persons. Let me tell you something else about rejection, and many have said this: the fear of rejection is always worse than the rejection itself. It still stings a bit, sometimes more so than others, but it's something that you're going to need to come to terms with to move forward in life.

There is a great TED Talk about rejection by Jia Jiang. In the talk, he describes a scenario where he sets out to undergo as much rejection as possible for one hundred days. He does everything from asking complete strangers for money to asking the manager at his local Starbucks if he can be a "Starbucks greeter" and greet everyone who comes into the establishment. I recommend this talk highly, but I want to mention one of the takeaways: rejection isn't really that bad (I already told you that), and it really does (like most things) get easier the more you experience it.

Unfortunately, most of us live our lives in the exact place where we get rejected just enough to never get comfortable with it. We get rejected in a particular context. We realize that it's going to be just fine, that it wasn't so bad. We may even gain a resolve to move fearlessly forward in all similar situations in the future. But then time goes by and we forget all that. Then we face another situation, and the fear of rejection once again cripples us. Even if we follow through in whatever the situation might be, we face unnecessary and often sinful anxiety as we approach it.

I told you I've applied for a lot of jobs in my life, and I shared a couple of those specific instances with you—so you know I've been rejected. It's never fun, but in certain areas, you do learn to roll with the punches. Your fear of rejection is also directly proportional to the specific situation you're in. Applying for a job isn't so daunting, especially nowadays where everything is done online, but there are certainly other situations that can feel a lot more intense.[21] And by other situations, I mean situations involving interaction with other people, although to be sure, you can find yourself getting rejected in pretty much any context in life. Encouraging, eh? Just keep reading.

Some of the best lessons I've learned—such as personal growth, self-awareness, and sanctification—have come from dating experiences I've had. While there are probably multiple reasons for that, it likely has something to do with the fact that I've wanted to get married since the seventh grade. In fact, I would say that I really don't want anything more than that, and that has been my general disposition for as long as I can remember. For this very reason, God has used this area to help me grow as a person and as a Christian.

My official first date went pretty well. She was a nice girl. That's why I asked her out—duh! It went well enough to warrant a second date. The second date seemed to go pretty well, also, though apparently

---

21 Of course, I recommend doing whatever you can to separate yourself from the other applicants (sending a separate email, studying about the prospective company, finding a way to introduce yourself to the supervisor, etc.). This must be done tactfully, though. There is a fine line between being a go-getter and being annoying.

not well enough to warrant a third date. I remember getting the text message that basically said that things would not be going any further. I was on a hike in the park. The adrenaline rush I got over that text message basically turned me into an MI6 agent. You are welcome to laugh. I remember taking off in a dead sprint through the wooded trail, flying up hills and jumping over fallen trees, and it was really something pretty impressive, if I do say so myself. We really are *fearfully and wonderfully made* (Psalm 139:14). In the aftermath of it all, I marveled at the human body and all that it could do. I'm not sure I had ever physically pushed myself so hard. It was pretty cool, but I'd really be lying to you if I said I wasn't crushed.

I was rejected. You will be rejected. Will Smith got it right too. In his 1997 remake of the song "Just the Two of Us," he tells his son that "there ain't no pain like from the opposite sex." I know it was only two dates, but it still kind of stunk. Have you ever experienced rejection like that? There is a temptation to start getting introspective when these things happen. You may start asking yourself if you could have or should have done something differently. You might even have more vain thoughts, such as wondering if you're not attractive enough. But here's what I've come to understand, and here's what you need to understand as well: sometimes things just don't work out. Sometimes we just get rejected. There isn't always a reason, or at least a reason we're privy to. An assessment of your actions in such situations is prudent for future improvement and success, but morbid introspection and overanalysis (I have been known to analyze the possible indications of punctuation in a text message) is not the right approach.

What Rejection Is and Is Not

People generally give you the same advice in these types of situations, too, and that is, "Don't take it personally." This is the worst possible thing anyone could say to you, mostly because it's impossible not to take it personally. The truth is that rejection is, in fact, very personal. But I think what people usually mean when they say not to take it personally is to not take it *maliciously*. It is personal, but it's also *okay*. It's part of life, and rejection doesn't mean that someone has it out for you. I would tell you, too, that you should never be angry at someone for rejecting you, regardless of the context. If it is in a context such as this, you can't possibly justify anger toward someone for not reciprocating particular sentiments toward you, and you certainly can't ever justify anger toward God. Again, this is part of life. You ought not to fear rejection, and you ought not to be angry about it either.

I think what makes rejection hit so hard is the implication that it's a very real assessment of our value. If someone rejects us, it means they don't see us as being valuable for whatever context we're considering. Not everyone is going to see your value—or perhaps they will, but will still determine that you just aren't the right fit for the job or the relationship or whatever. "Mick, I think you're a good guy, but..." I remember going through a similar situation of rejection and being in a really bad way about it. I was talking to the Lord and I said, "Lord, You don't understand what it's like to be rejected." I don't exactly remember if I was even able to finish the sentence or not, but instantly Isaiah 53:3 came to my mind: *He was despised and* rejected *by men, a man of sorrows and acquainted with grief; and as one from whom men hide their faces he was despised, and we esteemed him not* (emphasis added).

Turn to the Lord

The Lord knows what it's like to be rejected. He was rejected during His earthly ministry and was eventually crucified. He has been rejected all throughout history, despite the goodness and the grace He shows to all mankind (John 3:19; Acts 14:17; 17:25), and He is rejected every single time we sin against Him. He is indeed well acquainted with rejection. Understanding that God is acquainted with such rejection can help us work through our own rejection. For one thing, as we've already mentioned, no servant is greater than his master (John 13:16), so we can expect to be rejected at times if Christ, our master, was Himself rejected. In another way, our confidence in prayer is strengthened, knowing that Christ knows what we're going through and is there to help us.

> *For we do not have a high priest who is unable to sympathize with our weaknesses, but one who in every respect has been tempted as we are, yet without sin. Let us then with confidence draw near to the throne of grace, that we may receive mercy and find grace to help in time of need. (Hebrews 4:15–16)*

So, because Christ knows what we're going through, we can all the more draw near to Him, and we have His promise that we will receive help in our time of need, not just with rejection, but with anything. In Christ, we can accomplish things and move through trials that we would not have been able to do in our own strength. This is truly an incredible promise and is one of the many privileges of being a child of God. To think that the Creator and Sustainer of the universe promises to help us in our time of need, that we may at any time draw near to His throne of mercy, should leave us astounded. This should leave us in a state of utter gratitude—not just gratitude, though, but also, even as verse 16 above says, *confidence* to face whatever is in front of us, confidence that we are not facing it alone or in our own strength, but in the strength of Him who is stronger than all. *The Lord is on my side; I will not fear. What can man do to me?* (Psalm 118:6).

To be sure, it is not a sin to be rejected, but it is in times such as these when we are, perhaps, most tempted to sin. We're tempted to sin directly in our response to such rejection. We might be tempted to be angry at God or angry at the person who rejected us. Paul David Tripp notes that "a desire for even a good thing becomes a bad thing when that desire becomes a ruling thing."[22]

---

22   Paul David Tripp, *New Morning Mercies: A Daily Gospel Devotional* (Wheaton, IL: Crossway, 2014), April 5.

Sinful responses to rejection are evidence that a "good thing" has become a "ruling thing." We're also tempted to sin indirectly in such instances by seeking our refuge and comfort in something other than God. I know that for me it's particularly easy to want to turn on the television and just drown out my problems rather than taking them to the throne of grace. What folly there is in such a response, especially after all we have considered about the promise of God in our drawing near to Him in our time of need.

Again, I have been rejected countless times in countless situations. You will be too. Some of these situations are easier to handle than others. Some you will shrug off and some will really eat at you. Be assured, though, that no matter what happens, if you belong to God, He always has your best interests in mind, even if you don't always see it. You won't always see it, either; especially in the throes of rejection. God is always there, though, and He is always for you. I can also personally attest to the growth that He's given me in this area just during the last year. I went from an overanalytical freak who was totally crushed in the face of rejection to a partially overanalytical freak who, though disappointed when things don't work out, continues entrusting myself to Him who does all things good and right (Genesis 18:25; 1 Peter 2:23).

Seriously though, rejection is a lot easier to handle when you're really trusting that God knows what He's doing and when you're continually assured of His goodness. Even though you aren't necessarily getting what you want at the moment, you come to see more and more that He really is sufficient. You kind of just sit back and say, "Okay, Lord, I don't quite understand this one, but You're the boss and You know what You're doing." Keep that in mind as you face the rejection that will inevitably find you.

Journey well.

CHAPTER 5:
Set Goals and Make Sure You Plan

A man who does not plan long ahead
will find trouble at his door.
—Confucius

*Y*ou have to set goals, and you have to plan. I have to confess that for the vast majority of my years on this planet, I've never really even considered planning my life out. Things come up and, without even realizing it, you just end up going with the flow. You get up every morning. You go to school for a while, and then you go to college for a while. Then, if things go well, you get a job that matches up with your degree. Then you work that job, and you just keep going on that way. Let me tell you, too, that it happens in the blink of an eye. Before you know it, you've graduated from high school or college, and then, quite surreally, you find yourself in a completely different demographic. Just the other day I was reading an announcement about a "college-age Bible study," and I just sat there for a moment and realized, "Yeeeaaah, that's not me anymore." Life really is a vapor (James 4:14).

If you're not careful in life, you will go on autopilot, and like the mist that James mentions, your life will pass you by without you even realizing it. What's worse is that if you've failed to plan, if you've failed to go after what you want, the time that has passed will have afforded you nothing. As our lives pass us by, we should have something to show for them. God has us here for a reason. The stewardship that we've been given needs to be taken seriously. I tremble at what my standing before God will look like if I don't try to do something with all that He has taught and given me.

While we often waste time on autopilot, much of our wasted time comes from worrying about the past. You can't change the past. You must look at such mistakes, failures, shortcomings, and missed opportunities and embrace the fact that all those things have made you who you are. Learn from them. Make them worthwhile. Get a return on your investment from them, but realize you can't erase them. The sooner you come to terms with that and move on with your life, the better things will go for you. Sometimes, though, that's the toughest part of walking by faith in this life. We really need to trust, and we really can trust, that God has taken care of all our mistakes and all our sins. He nailed them to the cross (Colossians 2:14). It's not our job to try to cancel those things out. Christ already did that on our behalf. Walking by faith means trusting in that, resting in that, and moving forward with a holy disposition to the glory of God.

You can't just keep getting by on autopilot, because if you do that, somewhere along the way, something you're overlooking—called *life*—actually happens. Things don't always go smoothly. The truth is that even as I write this, I struggle with heeding this important life principle of planning, of really sitting down and deciding what I want to do, so long as the Lord permits, and then actually doing what I need to do to achieve that. This is a really simple concept, but it requires some work. It requires digging deep within yourself and answering some hard questions. You must consider some very real possibilities and embrace some essential, and likely uncomfortable, changes. Yes, that's hard, and it's why most people, myself included, tend not to sit down and work through such things.

Active Living, Not Passive Living

Here's a simple example for you. What's your favorite television show? Go! I bet you thought of the answer pretty quickly, or at least you thought of a few shows to pick from. Here's another example: Why are you here? What has God uniquely called you to do in this life? What do you want to do with your life? I guess that's technically three questions, but in some sense they're all the same, because as long as you can do what you want to do for His glory, God gives us our desires too. If you want to be a surgeon and you just can't think about doing anything else with your life, that is from God. The same goes if you want to be a writer. You just have to use discernment. If you have a desire to be something dishonorable or to go about getting something in a dishonorable way, you need to distinguish between your own carnal desires and what God would have you do. Those can be tricky questions sometimes. The good news is that God has given us a sufficient Word to test all things, and He has given us a church with whom we can seek counsel (Proverbs 11:14; 1 Thessalonians 5:21; 1 John 4:1).

You need to sit down and figure out the answers to those questions. People love to say things like, "You're still young," "You've got time to figure it out," or "It'll all work out." Well, my twenties disappeared in a flash, and let me tell you, it didn't all *just work out.*

You can't live life passively like that. That approach inevitably makes you a victim to the next set of circumstances, whatever they might be. As I look at my life over roughly the past decade, the truth is that I've largely been doing nothing but entertaining a myriad of passing fancies—moving on to the next best thing over and over and over again, ultimately turning myself into a troubled hamster running aimlessly on the wheel of life.

Planning and Goal Setting

Have you ever heard the expression, "If you fail to plan, you plan to fail"? It's true. It's very foundational, but I didn't see it for a long time. No one ever told me to sit down and plan my life out, to set a goal, to really figure out what I'd like to do and where I'd like to go. Or—kind of a testimony to the necessity of writing this book—maybe they did, but I obviously didn't listen too well. You need to set goals and make a plan. As Christians, we recognize that God is ultimately in control of everything and that we are to submit in advance to whatever He would have come our way in life. But that doesn't mean we just sit around and wait for things to happen to us. Yet how many live like that, or rather, how many *exist* like that? Because that's not really living at all.

For a long time after I stopped teaching, I was drifting. I hit some major lows. If I was out in public and spotted someone I hadn't seen in a while, I'd avoid them because I knew they'd inevitably ask me what I was doing with my life. I didn't want to have to answer them—because the truth is that I wasn't really doing anything. When avoidance didn't work, I could see the incredulity in people's eyes: "*This* is what's become of you?" Some people offered nice, encouraging sentiments, but the truth was that I wasn't satisfied with where my life was. I knew I could and should be doing more. John Wooden said, "Don't measure yourself by what you've accomplished, but rather by what you should have accomplished with your abilities."[23]

The first thing you need to do is set a goal. Set a goal and then write it down! You should have goals for everything. You should always have something in the crosshairs and know what you're after and why you're after it. You will, of course, have short-term goals and long-term goals. As I'm writing this book, for example, I might have goals regarding what I would like to accomplish in

---

23   John Wooden and Steve Jamison, *Wooden: A Lifetime of Observations and Reflections On and Off the Court* (Lincolnwood, IL: Contemporary Books, 1997), 94.

a sitting, and then I have a projected timeframe for when I want to have the whole thing done. Goals are great things and they are necessary things, and you should have some and stick to them.

Dr. John Street, one of my professors and a great leader in the Christian church today, says this about goals: "It's amazing to me how many pastors and just general Christian people don't understand the importance of goals in the Scripture.... Why is it that we must have goals? That's not a secular idea; that's a godly idea. Goals are nothing but ideas about how we want to achieve something that we're going about to achieve."[24]

When I was pretty far from the Lord and was eating up all kinds of self-help stuff, I really began to see that every single successful person I followed had goals or talked about goals. I saw that it was clearly necessary to set goals, but it wasn't until I had already determined to write this book that I came to realize just how much God has to say about setting goals and planning one's way to achieve them. You may have noticed by now that I talk about goals and plans kind of interchangeably, and that's because you can't really functionally have one without the other. What, then, does the Bible actually have to say about such things?[25]

> *The wisdom of the prudent is to discern his way,*
> *but the folly of fools is deceiving. (Proverbs 14:8)*

"Prudent" means wise or careful. We might use the word "cautious" here as well.[26] God praises the one who is discerning, the one who makes good judgments about his way. And what is his way, but the means of achieving his goal? We might even say

---

24   John D. Street, "Lecture 4: Marriage and Family Counseling" (lecture, The Master's Seminary, March 4, 2012), https://www.youtube.com/watch?v=BqWhAKgEItA&list=PLF0AB643DC4B01A1B&index=5&t=0s.

25   The majority of verses in this section were referenced and taken from Dr. John Street's lecture on marriage and family counseling, as referenced above.

26   Jay Adams uses this word in his translation in *Christian Counselor's Commentary: Proverbs* (Woodruff, SC: Timeless Texts, 1999), 106.

it is his course or his plan. A planned way, a way that has been carefully thought through, is a wise way and is in contrast to the way of the fool. It's easy to fall into a pattern of moving forward, thinking you're moving in a good direction, only to figure out later that such wasn't the case. Jay Adams writes, "It is a sad note that many foolish persons plunge headlong into bad decisions, get involved in sinful ways, and pursue empty dreams simply because they lack *caution*."[27] Such folly can be deceiving, but planning and discernment can guard us against such foolishness.

> *Every prudent man acts with knowledge,*
> *but a fool flaunts his folly. (Proverbs 13:16)*

Again, in this verse, we're shown that the prudent man acts according to knowledge. Such a man discerns, plans, and spends time thinking about things and working through things. He makes sure he has all the pertinent information before acting, and he allows that information to inform his actions. He looks at things from different angles and assesses the possible outcomes. We might say, commensurate with the words of Christ in Luke 14:28, that he *counts the cost*. He assesses all parts of the situation, which includes an assessment of himself.

Prioritize

Jim Rohn, America's foremost business philosopher and one of my favorite teachers, says this: "I often look at my life and ask, 'Well, here's what I want, but am I willing to become the kind of person it will take?' If I'm too lazy, if I'm not willing to learn, read, study, and grow to become what I must become, then I cannot expect to attract what I want. Now, when faced with a choice, I

---

27   Adams, *Christian Counselor's Commentary*, 106.

must decide to either change myself or change my wants."[28] What self-assessment needs to be done in your life? Have you counted the cost of the things you want to achieve? These are the actions of the prudent and of the wise.

> *Prepare your work outside;*
> *get everything ready for yourself in the field,*
> *and after that build your house. (Proverbs 24:27)*

This passage refers to the necessity of having priorities. When we set goals and plan things, prioritization always comes into play. Some things are more important than other things, or at least they should be. We have to make decisions according to our priorities. What are we valuing the most? God says here that you should tend to your field before your house. Or to say it another way, you should prioritize your fieldwork because it is contingent upon the seasons and the times. You can't just go do it whenever you want; you have to seize the moment and act. A house, though, you can build anytime. Prioritize things correctly so you can get everything accomplished and yield optimal results.[29]

We often like to think that we don't have time to do certain things we ought to be doing, but the truth is that we always make time for what we consider important and for what we prioritize. If you had a completely jam-packed schedule and someone came up to you and said you could receive 90 percent off everything in any store of your choosing, you'd somehow make time to be there, even amid your crazy schedule. How does that happen? Because you suddenly prioritized it. I have stopped using the phrase "I don't have time" with myself and with others because I have the

---

28   Jim Rohn, *Seven Strategies for Wealth & Happiness: Power Ideas from America's Foremost Business Philosopher* (New York: Three Rivers Press, 1996), 41.

29   John D. Street, "Lecture 4: Marriage and Family Counseling." Although Dr. Street's explanations of the selected passages were foundational to my use of them in this section, his explanation on this passage was particularly helpful.

same twenty-four hours every day that everyone else has. It's not about not having time; it's about how we choose to spend our time.

Let God and the Scriptures Guide Your Plans

Christians are commanded to make the most of their time, to seize the time, and to use the time wisely (Ephesians 5:15–16). Part of using our time wisely means working to ensure that we spend our lives pursuing godly desires in a thoughtful and prudent way.

> *Desire without knowledge is not good,*
> *and whoever makes haste with his feet misses his*
> *way. (Proverbs 19:2)*

This is a superb proverb and one that really hits home for me in a lot of ways. This verse recognizes that we all have desires—not necessarily good or bad desires, though we tend to have a mix of both. But the question here is whether our desires are *informed* desires. This goes back to our consideration of mindset and of thinking biblically. Are our desires informed by Scripture? This implies studying and planning. It implies the actions of the wise and prudent that we have been discussing. Such tactful considerations are contrasted with one who's always in a rush to do something, someone who *makes haste with his feet*. This is the person who just kind of goes with the flow, who always jumps at the first thing that pops up. This is how I would describe my own disposition throughout most of my life. If something sounded good, I just kind of did it. I didn't plan, I didn't think, and I didn't pray. I just acted hastily. God says such a person misses his way.

> *The heart of man plans his way,*
> *but the LORD establishes his steps. (Proverbs 16:9)*
> *Many are the plans in the mind of a man,*
> *but it is the purpose of the LORD that will stand.*
> *(Proverbs 19:21)*

These two verses go together, and actually, for a long time I was calling Proverbs 19:21 my life verse. That's because over and over again, in just about every context of my life, God has shown me that all the things that I thought I knew, that I thought I wanted, that I thought were right—were all wrong and that I actually knew nothing.

Sometimes it doesn't matter how diligently or prudently we've planned or how badly we want something. Sometimes God means for something else to happen. Even the wise who have planned diligently and have planned with knowledge are subject to this verse and this reality.

This reminds us of our place in the grand scheme of things. We aren't the authors of our lives, despite what all the motivational and self-help stuff out there would tell you. God is the author of our lives. We are active characters in *His* story, and He gives us a lot to enjoy as we move from page to page (1 Timothy 4:4–5), but we are always subject to His plan. It is our duty to humbly submit to Him, even when we would rather see the story go a different direction.

Jim Rohn asks, "Why won't you get everything you want? Because, my friend, it's not that kind of world. Sometimes it will hail on your crop and rain on your parade. Sometimes the termites of life will gnaw at your foundations. It's not fair, you say? Perhaps not. But because you and I were not consulted in the initial planning, we have to accept the way it is."[30] Proverbs 16:9 just further emphasizes this point. We might be the ones doing the planning, but our temporal plans all fit into God's eternal plan in such a way that He is the one who is actually establishing our steps—just as when Jesus told His disciples that although they thought they were choosing Him, He was really choosing them (John 15:16).

I hope you've come to see the wisdom in planning things out and in applying these verses and principles to your life. But it's not enough to simply have goals and to plan. There are a lot of people out there who know well enough what they *ought* to

---

30   Rohn, *Seven Strategies*, 48.

do but never actually do it. There is folly in that as well. In fact, someone who knows what to do and doesn't do it is the very definition of a fool. This is clearly illustrated in the parable Jesus told in Matthew about a wise man and a foolish man (Matthew 7:24–27). Jesus's emphasis here demonstrates the folly of *hearing* His words. That is, it shows the foolishness of *knowing* that what He said was right and knowing what should be done, but then not actually doing it. Jesus said such a person is like a fool who built a house on the sand. It doesn't exactly take a rocket surgeon to know that such an endeavor is not going to end too well. We have to set goals and make plans, but we also have to act on those plans. Such is the consideration of the next chapter.

Journey well.

CHAPTER 6:
Take Action and Keep Taking Action

It's a terrible thing, I think, in life to wait until you're ready. I have this feeling now that actually no one is ever ready to do anything. There is almost no such thing as ready. There is only now. And you may as well do it now. Generally speaking, now is as good a time as any.
—Hugh Laurie

*Y*ou have to take action, and you have to keep taking action. I took ballroom dancing lessons for about a year. One of the instructors there was from Kazakhstan. For one of our guest parties, I decided to bring my family, and my sister approached this dance instructor and asked how he came to be here, as anyone from my small town of Youngstown might wonder. With a heavy accent befitting his birthplace, he said, "Well, I wanted to dance in America, so I typed in 'dancing' on the internet. Youngstown popped up, and here I am." I might be simplifying that a little bit, but to my understanding, not much. What do you think of that? Kind of crazy, right? I don't think it's the fact that he traveled thousands of miles to be here that elicits a response of incredulity, but it's the simplicity of his answer. In some undetectable way, our brains are laughing because they've been conditioned to think that a big decision like that could not possibly be that simple. We've been conditioned to think that such things are beyond us. But they really *can* be that simple, and they're often not beyond us. They simply require us to take action.

All of the people who are doing the things they want to do and are achieving the things they want to achieve are people who took action. Think about it. Who's the best actor in the world? The best actress? The best singer? The best athlete? Are we to believe for a moment that there aren't better people out there, people we've never heard of, people we will never hear of? Of course there are better people out there! What is the difference between the people who are doing exactly what they want to be doing and those who aren't? The answer is (generally speaking) that those who achieved what they wanted took action at some point. They went for it. In life, you have to go for it! Go up to any married couple whose relationship you respect and whom you'd like to emulate in your own relationship, and ask them how they came to be married. I guarantee that at some point, no matter who you ask, the story will involve the woman being asked out and eventually proposed to. That man took action! Action is necessary to achieve the goals we set and to execute the plans we contrive.

Entrepreneur Gary Vaynerchuk gives some sobering insight about taking action and going for it in life:

> *I have no understanding as to why, when you're 18 to even, let's say 30, why you wouldn't try to make what you're passionate about work for you. If you go and become a lawyer or go to school and do all the things that everybody wants you to do, and don't do the thing you really love, the real question isn't what's going to happen when you're 23, 27, 31, 36. The question really becomes what's going to happen when you're 70 years old and you look back at your life and you're like, why didn't I try? There's going to be*

> *a regret factor that I think a lot of times a guidance*
> *counselor or parent or teacher tend not to think about.*
> *They're worried about your next ten years. I'm worried*
> *about your last ten years. And in those last ten years,*
> *you're going to be thinking back and realizing, why*
> *didn't I go to Austin or LA or Nashville or wherever*
> *you're going? Why didn't I take a chance? And really*
> *regret that. And that—that tastes a lot worse than*
> *going for it, because that's when you're most alive.*

There is a lot of truth in what Gary says here. Furthermore, he recognizes that sometimes your passions might take you in a different direction or to different places than others in your life think you should go. It's important to recognize this and to consider their words nonetheless, even if you don't end up doing what they think you should do.

> *Where there is no guidance, a people falls,*
> *but in an abundance of counselors there is safety.*
> *(Proverbs 11:14)*

Do you see the tension here? We need the wisdom of the people whom God has providentially put in our lives (again, the whole point of this book). We ought to put a lot of value in the wisdom that those more learned and more experienced seek to give to us. We ought to value the insight of godly people (Proverbs 19:20; 20:18). But at the end of the day, we're responsible for our own decisions. Others are not always going to understand, but they don't always have to. We have the freedom to walk our own path, as long as we're not sinning, but we will be responsible for the consequences of our actions. So we must choose wisely.

Gary basically says, "Go for it!" I can tell you, too, that life is so much more enjoyable and fruitful for me when I "go for it." I can also tell you that this really should have been my mindset all along. It's never too late to start, mind you, but again, the whole premise of this book is for you to learn such lessons—lessons I wish I would have realized much sooner.

Don't be discouraged if you've been living in fear and timidity and have allowed such things to paralyze you. I'm currently writing this book, I decided to take some cello lessons, and I even went horseback riding for the first time! God has given us so much here to enjoy—so enjoy it, with thanksgiving, giving Him the glory (1 Timothy 4:4–5). Don't get hung up on your past mistakes. Jim Rohn says:

> *My friend, there is nothing you and I can do about the past. It's gone and buried. But you can do a great deal about your future. You don't have to be the person you were yesterday. You can make changes in your life— absolutely startling changes in a fairly short period of time. You can make changes you can't even conceive of right now, if you just give yourself a chance.*[31]

I would say this is particularly true of Christians since the change that God enables us to make is the only true and permanent change that really exists. Remember, though, that "going for it" doesn't mean living life in such a way that aims to suck every bit out of it at the expense of faithfulness to God and at the expense of functionally living with an eternal perspective. It doesn't mean acting rashly and living like this world is all there is. We need a proper perspective here. We have to always keep Christ first (Exodus 20:2–3; Luke 14:26). If we aren't careful, we can easily fall prey to a disposition that makes the things of this world, many of them good things, idols or ends unto themselves. John Calvin says:

> *All the things that make for the enriching of this present life are sacred gifts of God, but we spoil them by our misuse of them. If we want to know the reason*

---

31 Rohn, *Seven Strategies*, 42.

*why, it is because we are always entertaining the
delusion that we will go on forever in this world.
The result is that the very things which ought to be of
assistance to us in our pilgrimage through life become
the chains which bind us.*[32]

We have to be careful of these chains. We have to guard our
hearts (Proverbs 4:23), watch ourselves (1 Timothy 4:16), and always
make sure that our minds are set upon Christ (2 Chronicles 12:14).

Tackling Fear to Get Out of Your Comfort Zone

The principle of taking action is closely related to the principle of
the comfort zone we've already discussed. Taking action requires
stepping outside your comfort zone. In fact, to take it a step further, I would almost say that the very definition of taking action
is *really* stepping outside your comfort zone. The same things that
generally prevent people from extending themselves are the same
things that prevent people from taking action: fear and laziness.

We tend to fear much in life. We might fear the outcome
of a particular endeavor. We might also fear failure. Failure isn't
something to fear, though. I can't express this point enough. Failure
is often good, for even when we don't succeed, we nevertheless
learn. If you're afraid to fail, you'll never accomplish anything in
life. Russell Brunson, the internet marketing guru of our day, gives
some extremely practical advice about overcoming fears in such
scenarios.[33] He basically says you need to get comfortable with
the worst-case scenario. He says that until you become okay with

---

32   John Calvin, *The First Epistle of Paul the Apostle to the Corinthians*, trans.
John W. Fraser, New Testament Commentaries, vol. 6 (Grand Rapids: Eerdmans,
1960), 159.

33   Russel Brunson, "Being OK with the Worst Case Scenario" in
Marketing in Your Car, podcast, https://marketingsecrets.com/episode-12-
ok-worst-case-scenario.

that, you will be too scared to take a risk. So think of whatever situation you're in or whatever endeavor you're considering—and think about the worst possible outcome. Then ask yourself if you're okay with that. If you are, you can confidently move forward. You can take action! If you aren't okay with it, perhaps you need to hit the drawing board again. You need to count the cost (Luke 14:28).

Fear of man is also a big problem for a lot of people, including me. We're often too worried about what other people think of us. We're afraid of their judgment, we're afraid of awkwardness, and we're afraid of who knows details about our lives. Aside from such fear being a gross demonstration of pride, our fears are generally irrational. I remember one of my first dancing experiences. I was out on the dance floor with basically no clue what I was doing. I was frustrated and anxious, figuring that everyone around me, everyone in the whole place, was thinking about how bad I was. Then something great happened. I looked around and realized that nobody was paying any attention to me. We're so self-centered and self-consumed sometimes that we think we're the center of the universe. Oftentimes we fall into sin and actually *become* the center of our own universe, but we fail to realize that we aren't the center of anyone else's (because they're self-centered sinners too!). Don't live life constrained by what other people may or may not think.

Although such practical considerations are often helpful, as Christians we must also consider the theology behind such deliberations. We've explored this in some measure in considering comfort zones, but it's worth repeating here. Oftentimes the fear we experience and the anxiety that accompanies it is actually sinful. So aside from the fact that such irrational fear leads to laziness, paralysis, and staying within that stagnant comfort zone, it can also be a sin against God. In Matthew 10, Jesus teaches us how we are to view our fellow man in terms of being afraid of them:

> *And do not fear those who kill the body but cannot kill the soul. Rather fear him who can destroy both soul and body in hell. (Matthew 10:28)*

Jesus tells us here that we are not to fear people, but we are to fear God. The fear that we have for God ought to outweigh the fear that we have for anyone around us. This is also a command; it is not optional. What other people think should not stifle our course of action or dictate the direction of our life. God is the only one who should incite such fear in us. Believe it or not, Jesus speaks on this as well:

> *Therefore I tell you, do not be anxious about your life, what you will eat or what you will drink, nor about your body, what you will put on. Is not life more than food, and the body more than clothing? Look at the birds of the air: they neither sow nor reap nor gather into barns, and yet your heavenly Father feeds them. Are you not of more value than they? And which of you by being anxious can add a single hour to his span of life? And why are you anxious about clothing? Consider the lilies of the field, how they grow: they neither toil nor spin, yet I tell you, even Solomon in all his glory was not arrayed like one of these. But if God so clothes the grass of the field, which today is alive and tomorrow is thrown into the oven, will he not much more clothe you, O you of little faith? Therefore do not be anxious, saying, "What shall we eat?" or "What shall we drink?" or "What shall we wear?" For the Gentiles seek after all these things, and your heavenly Father knows that you need them all. But seek first the kingdom of God and his righteousness, and all these things will be added to you. Therefore do not be anxious about tomorrow, for tomorrow will be anxious for itself. Sufficient for the day is its own trouble. (Matthew 6:25–34)*

Three times in this passage, Jesus commands us not to be anxious; yet if we are honest with ourselves, how often do we allow our minds to run amuck? Anxiety has become an acceptable sin, and instead of taking our thoughts captive to Christ (2 Corinthians 10:3–5), we entertain the passing speculations of our hearts and enter into a downward spiral of anxiety that inevitably affects our disposition and has a powerful negative influence upon our actions. Jesus says we should not be doing this. That should be enough for us, but His teaching is actually quite practical too. All theology is practical, by the way (if properly understood and applied), but here especially Jesus tells us why we should not be anxious. He gives both a horizontal and a vertical consideration to the matter, justifying His command by using a temporal reality and an eternal promise.

In verse 27 Jesus asks who can add even an hour to his life by being anxious. He considers the temporal reality that all the worrying and anxiety in the world isn't going to do anything. It isn't going to make the situation any better. It isn't going to change what's happening. He then turns the attention of His listeners to the fact that they ought not to worry because God is not going to let anything ultimately happen to them. Using an argument from the lesser to the greater, He says that God takes care of the grass of the field, so how much more will He take care of you? We all have that same promise! This doesn't mean that things are always going to go our way, of course, but it does mean that the apostle Paul's words are truer than ever: *God, who did not spare His own Son, but gave Him up for us all, will also with Him graciously give us all things* (Romans 8:32). That *all things* is pertaining to anything that is needed to make us more like Christ and fulfill His promise to bring us into His glorious kingdom.

So, then, we have no reason to fear. We're in the protective custody of the Father.

Persistent Action with God's Help

In the same way that it's not enough to just set goals and plan for them, it's still not enough to just take action, but we must also *keep taking action*. Grant Cardone said that "persistence is the single most common trait of the most successful."[34] Most people, though, give up on their goals as soon as things get a little difficult. I've heard that disposition likened to blowing a tire, pulling over to the side of the road, and slashing the other three tires. Jesus also, albeit in a different context, talks about the dire consequences of allowing adversity to stop you from continuing (Matthew 13:21). He was speaking of salvation, of those who fall away because of persecution on account of the Word of God, but this sentiment is axiomatic. You're not going to get anywhere if you quit when things get hard. I've failed so many times in my life. I've given up on many things, too, and when I wasn't failing and giving up, I was just sitting around waiting for something to fall into my lap. This is a terrible, unproductive, and unfaithful way to go through life.

There's a group of professing Christians out there who like to trumpet the mantra "Let go and let God." In some sense, I understand that they're trying to communicate their trust in a sovereign God, but in all honesty, that's also a horrible way to go about things, and it will lead to a lot of frustration. Our God is a God of means. Things don't just happen as if by magic. The biblical principle of reaping and sowing applies. I used to tell my Bible students that they could sit in a chair for hours upon hours praying that they would do well on an exam, but if they didn't actually put in the work and go study, all the praying in the world wouldn't likely result in a solid performance on the test. Again, God is a God of means.

The same principle applies to those seeking employment. You can pray that the Lord will bring you a job, but generally speaking,

---

34   Grant Cardone, *10x Quotes* (Cardone Training Technologies, Inc., 2014), 37.

if you don't go and fill out applications, no one's just going to decide to call you out of the blue. Even regarding looking for a spouse, Proverbs 18:22 says, *He who finds a wife finds a good thing.* Finding something, of course, presupposes that you were looking for it in the first place. And why wouldn't you be looking? Why wouldn't you be taking action? The reasons are likely fear, laziness, and an infatuation with the comfort zone. You can't claim ignorance, either, especially in our day and age. We have the world at our fingertips. If you don't know something, it's no one's fault but your own—especially if you're reading this book!

Matt Smethurst wrote, "As J. I. Packer once put it, 'The Christian's motto should not be 'Let go and let God' but 'Trust God and get going.'"[35] Don't be like the sluggard:

> *Go to the ant, O sluggard;*
> > *consider her ways, and be wise.*
> *Without having any chief,*
> > *officer, or ruler,*
> *she prepares her bread in summer*
> > *and gathers her food in harvest.*
> *How long will you lie there, O sluggard?*
> > *When will you arise from your sleep?*
> *A little sleep, a little slumber,*
> > *a little folding of the hands to rest,*
> *and poverty will come upon you like a robber,*
> > *and want like an armed man. (Proverbs 6:6–11)*

How long will you lie there before you take action? "Apathy is a spiritual killer,"[36] a lazy Christian is a contradiction, and no sluggard will keep the commitment and execute the discipline necessary to do anything in this life.

---

35   Matt Smethurst, "5 Christian Clichés That Need to Die," *The Gospel Coalition*, March 28, 2017, https://www.thegospelcoalition.org/article/5-christian-cliches-that-need-to-die/.

36   Borgman, "The Parable."

No Regrets

When I was in my early twenties, I wanted to be an actor. Don't laugh. I wanted to be an actor, and I wanted it for all the wrong reasons. I had no experience acting and I didn't have any reason to like it, but I knew that if I were an actor I'd have fame, wealth, and my own glory. These were terrible motivations, but I went after it. I took action. I signed up for a film school, flew out to Los Angeles to scope things out, and lined up a place to live in North Hollywood. Then I packed up my car and drove 2,400 miles across the country to make it big. How long did I live in North Hollywood? Now you can laugh. Two days. I never even unpacked my car!

I remember driving around southern California crying. Actually, I was sobbing. It's okay to cry, by the way, but it's not okay to quit.[37] I had no clue what I was doing. I just knew I wasn't willing to make the necessary adjustments to live out there. I gave up. I got my oil changed at a Walmart in Valencia, drove thirteen hours to Santa Rosa, New Mexico, stayed the night, and then drove twenty-three hours straight home to Canfield, Ohio. Actually, I remember getting off the highway in the wrong place, still about forty minutes or so from home. All I had in my stomach was a bag of Tostitos and two Monster energy drinks. I recall being hunched over the steering wheel with the empty bag of chips in my hand in case I succumbed to the nausea. That wasn't fun.

However, I don't regret that experience. I don't regret anything in my past—because everything in my life now is a result of everything that preceded. The same is true for you! I've had experiences and I've met people I otherwise wouldn't have had or

---

37 I say this in the present context of emphasizing the general need to persist and persevere in life. Sometimes, the best thing to do in a particular situation is quit and go a different direction. This is reminiscent of some of what we touched on in Chapter 2. Whether we need to persist and try harder or quit and move on to something else is a matter of wisdom. Life is full of these types of dilemmas.

met, and I wouldn't trade any of that. This California experience in particular, I believe, was the catalyst to my coming to a saving faith in Jesus Christ and becoming a Christian, and that's the most important thing that has ever happened to me. It's the most important thing that could ever happen to anyone.

God has worked all my mistakes and shortcomings out for good, and if you're honest about your own difficulties and mistakes, you'll see that they've made you who you are as well. How could we have regrets if God has promised to work out all things for our good (Romans 8:28)?[38]

Ignore the Voices

Even with such an outlook, we still need to learn from our experiences. I gave up. I need to warn you here, too, that the more you start stepping out and going for the things you want in life, the more you're going to start to hear voices.[39] I don't mean that pursuing your goals is going to somehow turn you into a schizophrenic or something, but you start hearing voices. What do the voices say?

"Give up!"

"Take the easy way out!"

"People will think you're foolish."

The toughest thing about a lot of those voices is that they sometimes hit awfully close to home and cripple us from moving forward. We too often succumb to doubt and fear instead of doing what we want to do.

---

38   "The 'good' in this context does not refer to earthly comfort but conformity to Christ (v.29), closer fellowship with God, bearing good fruit for the kingdom, and final glorification (v.30)." *The ESV Study Bible* (Wheaton: Crossway, 2008), 2171.

39   Les Brown talks about the importance of winning the inner dialogue. His teaching was foundational for my writing in this section. https://singjupost.com/les-brown-stop-negative-thinking-believe-full-transcript/?singlepage=1

Some of those questions are part of my own battle, too. That's why I am writing this book—in order to hopefully spare you some of that. The truth is that just about every night I wonder if everything I've written that day is just a pile of garbage, but I'm not succumbing to my old way of doing things. I'm going to press on, and I hope that's an encouragement for you to press on as well.

You need to win that inner dialogue with yourself, to beat down that inner voice that says,

"Oh, I could never do that."

"Oh, I'm just not ready."

"Oh, that'll never work out."

"Oh, it's just not the right time."

Whatever it might be, don't listen to those voices! You have to beat them down, you have to keep going, and you have to do it right now! Don't let them talk you into "getting started *tomorrow*" because if that's your mindset, tomorrow tends to never come. J. C. Ryle rightly recognizes tomorrow as "the devil's day."[40] We need to be a *today* kind of people.

Without planning, goals, action, and perseverance, you become passive in life rather than active—a slave to the next set of circumstances. You lose the ability to adequately discern what decisions to make, and you are unable to subsequently judge whether they were the right decisions. I can't believe it took me as long as it did to see that not having these things would ultimately result in never really achieving anything, at least anything I wanted. But I'm thankful because some people never realize that. You all know those people. They're here just existing, going through the motions, not doing what they want to be doing, and not achieving what they know they're capable of.

Our main purpose here is to glorify God, but what that looks like and how we do that is something serious we need to work toward and plan for. So don't nestle into a groove of complacency.

---

40   J. C. Ryle, *Thoughts for Young Men: Addressing the Greatest Challenges in a Young Man's Life* (San Antonio: The Vision Forum, Inc., 2001), 5.

Don't run the rat race, even if you're enjoying a measure of success. If you're not living up to your potential, you know it, even if others don't. I'm here to tell you that you don't have to stay where you are. Set a goal, make a plan, and execute it. If you don't know how, find someone who knows how and who will help you. We can't always control the things that come our way, but we're responsible for how we handle them and what we do with what we've been given.

Dr. R. Albert Mohler, the ninth and current president of the Southern Baptist Theological Seminary, and also the youngest president of the same institution, was appointed to his office in 1993 at the age of 33. The seminary had fallen prey to the growing sentiments of theological liberalism that seemed pervasive in American evangelicalism at the time. Upon his appointment, Dr. Mohler wasted no time returning that Southern Baptist bastion of liberalism to its faithful theological roots, eventually turning the seminary into the mecca of evangelicalism that it is today—the flagship seminary of the Southern Baptist Convention and one of the largest seminaries in the world.

Amid overwhelming adversity on all sides, and by the grace of God, Dr. Mohler prevailed. One former seminary student recalls a conversation he had with Dr. Mohler during that tumultuous time. He said, "Dr. Mohler, these people here don't like you. They don't even want you here. Do you really think you are going to be able to turn this ship around?" Dr. Mohler answered, "I'm either going to turn this ship around, or I'm going to sink it."[41]

I try to live my life the same way—going for the things I want, unapologetically, in a way that honors God—and always by His strength. I implore you to do the same.

Journey well.

---

41   "Recovering a Vision: The Presidency of R. Albert Mohler, Jr." https://www.youtube.com/watch?reload=9&v=A1k9HyxLiOY.

CHAPTER 7:
Get Used to Disappointment

Often when you think you are at the end of something,
you're at the beginning of something else.
—FRED ROGERS

*Y*ou have to get used to disappointment. Life is full of it. Don't
let anyone fool you; things are not always going to go as
you'd like them to. Disappointment comes in all shapes
and sizes, and in God's providence, it has all kinds of different
purposes, some of which we're privy to seeing and some of which
we may not be. However, such purposes are always good, for they
come from the hand of Him who does only good (Psalm 119:68)
and who is goodness itself (Psalm 34:8). It's important for you to
understand this and to know how to respond appropriately when
disappointment inevitably comes.

I've worked in various positions within the education field over
the years, but at one point I had the privilege of teaching high
school Bible class at a Christian school. This was undoubtedly one
of the most fulfilling and enriching experiences of my life, and
I'm forever thankful to God for the time I got to spend with my
students and speak such important truths into their lives. It wasn't
just to their benefit, but it was certainly to my benefit as well.

Looking back, I see that they had more of an impact upon my life than I realized at the time. You'll find times like that, too, as you continue on your journey. You'll begin to see how very important people are and how very important relationships are. You'll begin to see that life is not so much about what you're doing, but about who you're doing it with. This is very practical, but it's also a sign of growth as we come to value relationships more and more. After all, we are relational beings by our very nature, having been made in the image of God, who is Himself an eternally perfect relationship—Father, Son, and Holy Spirit.

But interestingly, being young, zealous, and committed to the whole counsel of God (Acts 20:27), I seemed to be a bit of an outsider, even though I was at a Christian school. Sometimes in our desire to be seen as loving and accepting, we go too far and neglect God's truth. Perhaps that's what happened here. Even though I sought to be faithful to the message of Jesus, my beliefs didn't seem to align with those of the school. And so it was that on a Friday evening, after about two years of employment, I was called in by the administration and informed that I would not be returning to work on Monday. My boss was very nice about it and even honored my contract, paying me even though I wouldn't be working—but I was dismissed from my position just like that. I went to work that morning with a job, with an opportunity to speak into the lives of young people, and I went home that evening without either. This was disappointing, to say the least.

I had already told the school administration that I wouldn't be returning the following year, as I was planning on going to seminary (which you'll recall I didn't end up doing), but this was still very sudden. Let the suddenness of such change in my own life sober you to the reality of just how quickly things can change. I therefore implore you not to take anything, any opportunity, or any time that God gives you for granted. Remember the parable of the talents (Matthew 25:14–30)? We're stewards of everything that God graciously gives us, and we must make the most of it. We're not promised the status quo, and we will be held accountable for our use of what He gives us. This is a common theme not only in this book, but in all of life.

I have to confess that a part of me was initially kind of glad to be getting paid without having to show up to work. Somewhere along the way the incredible opportunity God had given me had become just a job to me, just something that I had to get done. I had grown complacent, and I had lost sight of how important the work was that I was doing. Then it was taken from me.

Perhaps the most difficult part of the whole thing was that I wasn't allowed to say good-bye to my students. I was there one day and gone the next. I'm thankful to the Lord, though, that the school still let me chaperone the senior class trips for the next several years. God taught me a lot through this experience, but His Word directly informed my response to such disappointment, and it also afforded me much comfort.

> *For to this you have been called, because Christ also suffered for you, leaving you an example, so that you might follow in his steps. He committed no sin, neither was deceit found in his mouth. When he was reviled, he did not revile in return; when he suffered, he did not threaten, but continued entrusting himself to him who judges justly. (1 Peter 2:21–23)*

If Christ, the sinless and perfect Son of God, was reviled, if He suffered wrong and yet did not retaliate, then how much more should I have a humble disposition in such a situation? It was not my job here to take revenge. It was not even my job to attempt to vindicate myself to anyone; but just as Christ did, my job in this situation was to continue entrusting myself to Him who judges justly. God had ordained this from before the foundation of the world. Somehow, this was for my good and for His glory.

Looking back, I can surely see that. I was made more like Christ through this situation. Regardless of the nature of your disappointment—perhaps something you really wanted to happen fell through, perhaps you've been wronged by someone, or, as we discussed in chapter 4, maybe you've been rejected and are working through that pain—it is such an encouragement to know that we have a just God who is good and faithful to whom we can entrust ourselves. What disappointments is God using in your life to make you more like His Son? What trials is God using to draw you nearer to Him? In what areas of your life is He calling you to trust Him more?

I'm so thankful I decided to write this book from a thoroughly Christian perspective because I don't know how I could ever explain how to handle such disappointments apart from God. Yet if you look around, the vast majority of the world is trying, without success, to do just that. Sure, things might be swept under the rug for a bit. People might muster enough gusto to ignore their plights and their mortality and try to mask their problems, telling themselves everything is fine and they're happy, but this is both farcical and futile. Mark Manson points out:

> *Highs come in many forms. Whether it's a substance like alcohol, the moral righteousness that comes from blaming others, or the thrill of some new risky adventure, highs are shallow and unproductive ways to go about one's life. Much of the self-help world is predicated on peddling highs to people rather than solving legitimate problems. Many self-help gurus teach you new forms of denial and pump you up with exercises that feel good in the short term, while ignoring the underlying issue. Remember, nobody who is actually happy has to stand in front of a mirror and tell himself that he's happy.*[42]

---

42   Manson, *The Subtle Art*, 33.

How to Deal with Disappointments

What is the answer to such disappointment? How can you get through it? The answer goes back to the very first chapter of this book. We need to consider our mindset when such disappointments come our way. We need to make sure we're thinking biblically both in analyzing a particular situation and in determining our response to it. There's much debate about how effective the Bible is in speaking to the problems we encounter in life, but it really is sufficient. It really does speak to the various issues that we all face in life, and it really does tell us how to respond to them (2 Peter 1:3). More than that, we who are Christians can be assured that by the power of the Holy Spirit within us, we can respond in a way that honors God despite how impossible such a response might seem under particular circumstances. And that which honors God best in a particular situation is always what is best for us.

As I think through some of the experiences in my life and some disappointments that seemed to occur as a result of remaining faithful to what the Bible teaches, I'm reminded of these words from one of my heroes of the faith, John MacArthur: "Never for a moment coming out of seminary did I think that I would spend most of my life, on the greater front beyond my church, trying to affirm the true gospel while under assault from so-called believers." This is the reality of the world we live in. Are you prepared to face it?

Furthermore, recall that the Bible says that such assaults would befall us if we're faithful (Psalm 34:19; 2 Timothy 3:12). The apostle Peter also refers to such tribulations and tells us we shouldn't be surprised when such things come our way as though something strange were happening to us, but that we should rejoice insofar as we share Christ's sufferings (1 Peter 4:12–13). What jumps out at you from that? How about the fact that Peter tells us we're to rejoice in our sufferings? When was the last time you were joyful because you were suffering? Has Peter lost it? Well if he has, so have a bunch of other authors of Scripture. James, for example, says, *Count it all joy, my brothers, when you meet trials of various kinds, for you know that the testing of your faith produces steadfastness* (James 1:2–3).

Again, are we really supposed to consider it a joyful thing when we encounter unfavorable circumstances? What's the deal here? The biblical authors aren't advocating that we should be happy when bad things happen to us or delighted that we're in pain, either emotional or physical, but rather they're applying the biblical mindset, and they're explaining things through those Bible-tinted glasses we mentioned. As Heath Lambert explains, when James says we should count our trials a joy, he isn't saying we should be joyful *at* our trials, but that we should be joyful *in* them; the preposition matters here, and it matters a lot.[43]

When disappointments come your way, you're not going to be happy about them. That's normal—it's human. It can even be right. But God has so provided for us that the whole point the biblical authors are making here is that we can be joyful *in* or *through* our trials *despite* what is happening around us. Our hope is rooted in eternity, not in the things of this world! God has promised us a rich inheritance that far surpasses anything we might hope for in this life—an inheritance that makes all of our sufferings and disappointments seem small in comparison.

This is what the apostle Paul meant (and think again of all the suffering he endured—2 Corinthians 11:16–33; 2 Timothy 4:6) when he said, *For I consider that the sufferings of this present time are not worth comparing with the glory that is to be revealed to us* (Romans 8:18). Having an eternal perspective, focusing on the character and purposes of God, and resting in His promises are the practical means whereby we, through His grace, can persevere through the trials of this life.

Here's what I'm not saying. I'm not saying you should take Bible verses like aspirin, popping a couple down the old gullet and hoping you'll be all good to go when you wake up in the morning. I'm also not saying that a right application of Scripture means you're going to automatically feel better, though sometimes God

---

43   Heath Lambert, "I Will Bear Witness," (lecture, CCEF National Conference, October 3, 2014), https://www.youtube.com/watch?v=-1yoWoY0KX4&t=460s.

does work that way. What I *am* saying is that as we begin to see things through the lens of Scripture, and as we begin to think God's thoughts after Him, we will actually begin to see things differently. It's very tempting to want to feel sorry for ourselves, but God would have us respond in a better way, and He gives us the grace to not be defeated by the problems we face.

Remember that God has, by His good hand, brought these things into your life. Nothing gets by Him. He *works all things according to the counsel of his will* (Ephesians 1:11), and He even tells us that sometimes it will be *necessary* for us to be grieved by various trials (1 Peter 1:6–7). We might not think it's necessary any more than a two-year-old doesn't think it's necessary for his parents not to let him eat his entire birthday cake in one sitting. But if we're honest with ourselves, we don't always know what is best for us any more than a toddler does. But God always knows what's best. Eating an entire cake would make anyone pretty sick, and a good parent keeps his child from that, even if it means some temporary disappointment for the child. How much more so does God know how to parent us, His children (Matthew 7:11)?

Whatever your situation is, you need to look at it through the lens of God's character and His promises. I don't mean to trivialize any of the problems we face by giving such general counsel, and I would always encourage seeking the help and comfort of someone who is godly and trustworthy, but this is where we need to start in handling our disappointments. Sometimes pride and embarrassment get the best of us and we try to handle things on our own, but I can't encourage you enough to seek the help of a friend when you find life getting you down.

That's why God has ordained the church. There's no such thing as a "lone Christian." We're here to help one another and to bear one another's burdens (Romans 12:15; Galatians 6:2). Not only should you go to such a person who helps to bear the burdens of others, but you should *be* such a person. I can't tell you how much help the simplest encouragement from others can be when we're going through trials. Some people are especially gifted in this area of encouragement. A woman from my church comes to mind who, without even realizing it, in God's providence, has made encouraging comments to me in the most needful of times. The reality of the way God has ordered His creation is seen yet again: *Anxiety in a man's heart weighs him down, but a good word makes him glad* (Proverbs 12:25).

That verse is so true, and I've seen it in my own life repeatedly. In the face of one particular disappointment, I was especially discouraged. I was speaking with a friend (actually we were texting; this was 2019, after all). He said to me, "Mick, you are the best man I know, and that's not a joke." I have a screenshot of that text message saved on my phone. What a great encouragement that was to me! Be such an encouragement to those around you. Look for opportunities to encourage others, and don't be ashamed if you need a bit of that encouragement yourself from time to time. God knew you would need encouragement when He ordained the means of the church.

To close out this chapter, I want to share a few passages that I like to run to when I'm burdened by heartache and disappointment. This is but a fraction of all the riches the Bible holds for us as we seek to live faithful lives in a fallen world and persevere through the hardships along the way.

You are good and do good; teach me your statutes (Psalm 119:68). Here the psalmist tells us plainly about the character of God. He is good. He is *always* good. He does good. He *always* does good.

We might not see the light of His goodness at the end of our tunnel of suffering, but this verse is a powerful reminder that God would never do anything unkind or unloving to us. He always acts perfectly and righteously. It is who He is. Keeping this in mind amid our suffering is a powerful means of perseverance. It's always a prudent response in life to run back to what you know to be true about God. He is good and He does good.

> *For the L*ORD *God is a sun and shield;*
> *the L*ORD *bestows favor and honor.*
> *No good thing does he withhold*
> *from those who walk uprightly.*

> *O LORD of hosts,*
>> *blessed is the one who trusts in you!*
>> *(Psalm 84:11–12)*

Oftentimes when we're disappointed, it's because things don't go our way; we want something we're not getting, or we're getting something we don't want. The psalmist here tells us that whatever we're being kept from, whether it's a relationship, a job, or good health—God is keeping you from something *for your good.* If it were good, you'd have it.

In all these things, God is able to do far more than we can ask or even think (Ephesians 3:20), and what we're asking or thinking generally falls short of what He has planned. C. S. Lewis said, "I am sure that God keeps no one waiting unless He sees that it is good for him to wait."[44] If you're meant to have that job or that relationship or whatever it might be, *nothing*, and I mean *nothing*, could possibly thwart the purposes of God in getting it to you (Job 42:2). You will have what He means you to have, when He means you to have it. And we already know He is good, so that should be a great encouragement to you. *No good thing does he withhold from those who walk uprightly* (Psalm 84:11).

> *My heart is in anguish within me;*
>> *the terrors of death have fallen upon me.*
> *Fear and trembling come upon me,*
>> *and horror overwhelms me.*
> *And I say, "Oh, that I had wings like a dove!*
>> *I would fly away and be at rest;*
> *yes, I would wander far away;*
>> *I would lodge in the wilderness;*
> *I would hurry to find a shelter*

---

44 C. S. Lewis, *Mere Christianity: A Revised and Enlarged Edition, with a New Introduction, of the Three Books, The Case for Christianity, Christian Behaviour, and Beyond Personality*, Macmillan paperbacks ed. (New York: Macmillan Pub. Co., 1984), 12.

> *from the raging wind and tempest."*
> *(Psalm 55:4–8)*

Here the psalmist describes some pretty intense suffering. Perhaps you've felt that way in the midst of your own trials. He's not mincing any words; in fact, he says that things are so bad that he wished he could fly away like a bird (verse 6). Have you ever wanted to just get away from your problems? Have things ever seemed so insurmountable that you believed there was no way out, that you would do anything to escape and just get away? You're in good company with the psalmist then. But notice how he perseveres. Notice where he turns. Notice how he applies a proper mindset as a balm to his hurting soul:

> *Cast your burden on the* LORD,
> *and he will sustain you;*
> *he will never permit*
> *the righteous to be moved. (Psalm 55:22)*

He takes his problems to the Lord, assured of the fact that he'll be safe there. You can do the same. In fact, that's what God wants you to do. Furthermore, many people like to think and believe that things are going to get better for them or that a "No" brings them closer to a "Yes," or any number of those one-lined clichés that they grab at in our Twitter-crazed age. But, those open doors and answers to our prayers don't always look the way we think they will, and only Christians have the promise that God is working out all things for their good (Romans 8:28). Only Christians can look confidently and hopefully to the road ahead, even in the midst of great suffering.

You'll notice that all the passages I've mentioned are found in the book of Psalms. That's certainly not the only place in God's Word that provides comfort, but the psalms are particularly rich. They're so very human, despite being divinely inspired. The psalmists are very honest about what they're going through, and it's very easy to relate to them as they express themselves in their writing.

Many times in my life I've been so enveloped by the sentiments of disappointment that I couldn't even utter a prayer. I prayed, mind you, but all I could say was, "Lord, help." And He did. He will. He does. Why? That's who He is, and that's what He has promised. He hears the prayers of the destitute (Psalm 102:17). He keeps you and will not let your foot be moved (Psalm 121:3). *He heals the brokenhearted and binds up their wounds* (Psalm 147:3). The children of mankind take shelter in the shadow of His wings (Psalm 36:7). He promises to keep in perfect peace those whose mind is stayed on Him (Isaiah 26:3–4). That is our God.

So know, then, that you will suffer in this life (Philippians 1:29). You will face disappointments. *But God* has a purpose in it, and you can always go to Him. *God is our refuge and strength, a very present help in trouble* (Psalm 46:1).

Journey well.

CHAPTER 8:
Be Successful

*I think everybody should get rich and famous
and do everything they ever dreamed of so
they can see that it's not the answer.*
—JIM CARREY

You have to be successful. More than that, God wants you to be successful. Perhaps that sounds a little questionable, but I purposely stated it in such a contentious way to get your attention. Let me explain. God does want you to be successful, but we need to recognize that how the world defines success and how God defines success are pretty much at opposite ends of the spectrum. The world defines success as who has the most stuff, the most fame, and the most money—as who is getting the most glory. But what the world esteems, God abhors (Luke 16:15).

We're surrounded by advertisements and propaganda that try to sell us the lives and the dreams of the rich, the famous, and the "successful." This is especially true in our internet- and social-media-crazed world where people are self-proclaimed entrepreneurs, influencers, YouTube stars, and the like. People make videos and take pictures standing in front of their mansions and their expensive cars with half-naked women, and they extend a hand and say, "This can all be yours." The masses jump at this kind of thing because they believe that's where they'll find satisfaction for all that their hearts long for. Theirs is an "if/then" mentality. They look at such things and say, "*If* only I had (fill in the blank), *then* I would be happy, *then* I would be satisfied, *then* I would be content."

That's why I love the quote above from Jim Carrey. He went out and made his dreams come true. He's rich, he's famous, and he has the life that most people dream of—most people's "if/then." Jim has all that, and he tells us it isn't the answer. I don't think we need to look too far to see that he's right, either. If you take just a cursory look at the latest smut-filled news coming out of Hollywood, you'll see that these superstars we all want to be like have lives filled with problems and drama, oftentimes more so than your average Joe. Jim Carrey is right. It's not the answer, yet it's an easy desire to be ensnared by; it's an easy path to go down. I've been tempted by such things often, blinded by a desire for worldly things, even as a Christian. We must be very careful. We must keep our guard up (Matthew 24:43; Revelation 16:15).

The apostle John warns us about loving the world and the things in the world:

> *Do not love the world or the things in the world. If anyone loves the world, the love of the Father is not in him. For all that is in the world—the desires of the flesh and the desires of the eyes and pride of life—is not from the Father but is from the world. And the world is passing away along with its desires, but whoever does the will of God abides forever. (1 John 2:15–17)*

Scripture recognizes that this is a danger, and we would do well to heed such a warning. The world promises a lot of things, but these are empty promises. The world doesn't have the answer. But I did tell you that God wants you to be successful, so what am I getting at here? Michael Horton, in his book *Ordinary*, shines a light on our dilemma:

Our passion for life and achievement and our desire to strive toward a daring goal are essentially hardwired into us by God. What has changed since the fall is the direction of this drive. Unhinged from its proper object—God's glory and our neighbor's good—our love becomes self-focused; our holy passions become vicious, driving us away from God's approaching steps and away from each other. We're not living in the real world, the creation that God called into being and sustains by the word of His power, but in a make-believe world. We are living as though God and our neighbors were made for us. In other words, we are living unnatural lives—living as if we were or could become someone other than the image of God, created to love God and each other.[45]

The problem here is that we've allowed the world to define success, and the world doesn't believe any of that. The world encourages everyone to chase after their dreams without regard for others. This isn't right. As Horton describes it, it's *unnatural*. Sadly, I don't think any of us realize just how influenced we are by the world. Whether we like to admit it or not, the world has affected us and our perception of what success looks like. Perhaps you scoffed a bit when I told you that "God wants you to be successful." This is evidence that you've been influenced by the world's definition of success. You, perhaps, deemed desire for success a bad thing. How could God want that for me? Well, if we think about success as the world thinks about success, then you'd be correct, but I think we let the world get away with too much if we let it so influence us. It doesn't get to do that.

---

45   Michael Horton, *Ordinary: Sustainable Faith in a Radical, Restless World* (Grand Rapids: Zondervan, 2014), 88.

But What, Then, Is Success?

Former UCLA basketball coach John Wooden has the best definition of success I've ever heard. He said that "success is a peace of mind that is the direct result of self-satisfaction in knowing you did your best to become the best that you are capable of becoming."[46] Write that down. I love his definition! It gives you permission to work for and achieve what you want rather than what someone else wants. It gives you permission to be content with what you have and where you're at because you're not necessarily always falling short of what someone else says you should have.

It means success isn't defined by whether you're wearing a Rolex or a Timex, if you're driving a Ford or a Ferrari, or if you fly coach or first class. It doesn't matter. This definition is why people selling you their dream is garbage. Now to be sure, their dream is not necessarily garbage. I personally think the sports car and the mansion aren't very substantive things to be living for (the Bible would advocate the same), but if that's what someone else is working toward and that's what they get, then they're successful according to Wooden's definition. There can be successful executives, entrepreneurs, doctors, and managers. There can also be successful plumbers, garbagemen, teachers, and waiters. Because success is subjective, it's directly related to what you're doing and what you're capable of, just as Wooden said. This is also reminiscent of our consideration of Romans 12:3 and the various gifts, abilities, and interests God gives to each of us.

Our culture rails against this concept as we're incessantly inundated with sentiments of discontentment. When I say we should strive to be successful, I mean that we should strive to be the best we can be according to the measure of grace God has given us to plausibly accomplish our endeavors. It's not meant to be an impetus

---

46   Wooden and Jamison, *Wooden*, 170.

to be on the ever-upward ascending elevator to the penthouse. We should be thinking like Snow White here, not Cinderella.[47]

Snow White spent herself for her companions in life. She was satisfied with her station and did her best to be successful, and she was. Even Grumpy would attest to that. Cinderella, on the other hand, *had* to date the prince. She *had* to break out of where God providentially had her. She sat around feeling sorry for herself. She had that "if/then" mindset, and she was thus a bad influence on the mice she often spoke to. That's not to say it would be wrong for Cinderella to better herself or her station in life. I mean, for real, her stepmother and sisters weren't exactly the kindest of people. The point here, though, is that Cinderella didn't seem content. She (and so many like her) thought she would find her ultimate joy and happiness in changing her station in life. Anyone, though, who has ever chased the ever-elusive "dream life" in all its varying forms will tell you that such just isn't the case. Think back to the words of Jim Carrey that we considered at the beginning of this chapter.

Although it seems like they're opposites, you can be content yet still desirous and working toward something you perceive to be better. When we have a right view of such things, we are thankful to the Lord for where He has us, yet prayerful for His grace and providence in moving us somewhere else. We should also thank Him for the gifts He's given us that make such endeavors a possibility, even if, in His wisdom, they never come to pass. Remember, Paul said that there is great gain in godliness with contentment (1 Timothy 6:6). That means that even if we lose what we're seeking (as if we ever really had it), God says we have gain if we're content in Him. Snow White never went to any royal ball, and she seemed to live a pretty happy life, the poisoned apple notwithstanding. Paul also says that if we have food and

---

47   I first heard this comparison mentioned by Voddie Baucham in his sermon, "What's More Important than a Wedding?" He mentioned reading it in an article entitled, "Stop Looking for a Wife, You Won't Find One," by W. F. Price. I've adapted it to fit the present context.

clothing, we should be content (1 Timothy 6:8). This flies in the face of our efforts to find ultimate satisfaction in whatever form our temporary pumpkin carriage might take.

Michael Horton discusses the discontentment our culture proliferates:

> *People who are perfectly content—truly happy—being janitors or gardeners are encouraged to become dissatisfied and restless. They should aim for the stars. Everyone should strive to work his or her way from the mail room to the boardroom. Even to question that, and to value neighbors simply for who they are in the civil body as well as the body of Christ, is considered condescending. Actually, though, isn't it less condescending to recognize the value of each person and his or her role in society and in Christ's body?*[48]

We Are Stewards

Being stewards means that success will look different for all of us. It means that God gives each of us different gifts, different abilities, and different opportunities—and how we use those things for His glory will look different. Recall again the parable of the talents. I know that we have referenced this teaching several times now, but it has many lessons for us as we consider how we're to be living faithfully in the here and now. The teaching of Jesus emphasizes a stewardship that all of us have been given (Matthew 25:14-30).

To summarize Tim Conway's teaching on this point: All of us are stewards over everything God has given us. We're stewards of our bodies, of our time, of our gifts, of our station in life, of our careers, of our singleness or our families—of everything. The parable also emphasizes the fact that the master is the one who

---

48   Horton, *Ordinary*, 97.

actually owned everything. Everything belongs to God. We don't so much own things in this life as much as we simply possess them for a time.[49]

So, to bring this full circle back to Wooden's definition, we should be doing our best with what God has given us, and if we do that, we can certainly have a peace of mind that, at least in this context, we're living faithfully to God. We needn't get discouraged that we don't have the same "talents" as someone else, for in God's system the rewards go not so much to the one who has the most, but to the one who has been faithful—you'll notice in Jesus's teaching that the servant who was given two talents and the servant who was given five talents were both praised in the same way.[50]

What do you think of all of that? Does that explain a bit of the tension in how you've thought about success? Are you satisfied with Wooden's definition? Really think about it. Are you? As I mentioned, I think Wooden's definition is a good one. In fact, it's very good. I would also reiterate that there really is a great degree of subjectivity concerning what success is. It's subjective insofar as it considers both our desires and our capabilities, which are different for everyone. But I think we need to take this a bit further. I don't think we can stop here and be faithful. I think there's an objective part of all this that we need to recognize.

Recall what we said concerning mindset. We said that a good mindset, or a good worldview, or good values, are defined as good by whether they align with what God says is good. So as we consider all our various gifts, abilities, and desires, and the subsequent endeavors that all those things may develop into, we have to stop

---

49   Tim Conway, "The Joy of the Lord" (sermon, San Antonio, Texas, August 2, 2015).

50   Borgman, "The Parable." In his teaching on this point, Borgman references a book by Kent and Barbara Hughes called *Liberating Ministry from the Success Syndrome.* He recalls Kent's words: "God's blessing is not necessarily on great gifts, it's on great faithfulness."

and consider whether our actions are something God would deem good and would view as successful.

Successful Motivations

Whatever our earthly endeavors are (and we should have earthly endeavors), they cannot rightly be called successful if they're not aimed at God's glory and if they're not achieved in a way that honors Him. Furthermore, they're ultimately meaningless and worthless if we live a life apart from Christ, die, and go to hell. *What does it profit a man to gain the whole world and forfeit his soul?* (Mark 8:36). The rich die the same as the poor.

A while back I wanted to be a public speaker. There is nothing inherently wrong with that, mind you. I really enjoy public speaking, teaching, and preaching. However, my motivations were not for the glory of God. I thought they were, but the truth is that they were full of worldliness and selfish ambition (James 3:14–16). I had begun following a bunch of entrepreneurs and the like on Facebook, and I pictured myself flying around the world in a private jet, speaking in front of large crowds, and making millions.

Sin, particularly worldliness, is very deceptive. I really thought I would be able to do all this to the glory of God. While my talks wouldn't be specifically *Christian*, I wanted to share the things I'd learned about life, and that was a good thing, right? Well, maybe it could be, but as the lessons I've learned—the lessons that have found their way into this book—have to do with how we live our lives as a whole (and that can't be rightly done without Christ), something never really sat right with me about it. I was in a difficult situation. Nothing I said or did was inherently sinful, but I knew the worldly motivations of my heart.

Paul Washer asks, "Why would we want fame when God promises us glory? Why would we be seeking the wealth of the world when the wealth of heaven is ours? Why would we run for a crown that will perish with time when we're called to win a crown that is imperishable?"[51]

By God's grace, a friend of mine challenged me about the path I was heading down. Again, he wasn't able to say I was actually doing anything wrong, but he just kind of matter-of-factly asked me what was going on. Clearly, the things I was saying and the philosophies I was purporting, though generally true, had a different taste than the things I was once so passionate about.

I needed to repent. There was more dissonance than ever in my thinking as I knew I had gone too far away from the gospel with many things, despite really wanting to better myself. Even after deciding to write this book, I still caught myself thinking, "How 'Christian' do I want to make this book? After all, I want it to sell. I want to write a best-selling book." I remember sharing some of my goals with another friend, and I'm compelled to share his response since it's universal in application (just like most of the lessons and experiences in this book). I trust it will benefit you as much as it benefitted me. It's a bit lengthy, but worth considering:

> *The Enemy is very subtle. And it is very common for him to take a positive intention and sneak his way into it, twisting the person's mind while having him still convinced he is doing what God wants. I think for pastors this is an especially huge temptation, and one that I constantly see people falling into without realizing it. They want a bigger church, a fancier production team, to look better on camera, and without even realizing it, they have applied worldly wants to what was originally just a desire to please God instead of others and themselves.*

---

51   David Jeremiah, *Discovering God: 365 Daily Devotions* (Carol Stream: Tyndale House Publishers, 2015), 264.

And when you say, "I once was tempted by worldly things, but now I just want financial freedom and to have a best-selling book," I would encourage you to go deep in prayer and ask God to reveal to you: are you really as "over" the temptation of the world as you believe? Is it possible that as a result of all the progress you have made thus far, you have come to a new layer of inward temptation without realizing it? And most of all, I would pray for discernment to see whether this is really a challenge for you to over-come—or perhaps a cross for you to bear in order to bring you more fully into humility and self-denial. I do not know whether it is one way or the other, but I do believe that oftentimes we can convince ourselves that we are supposed to achieve something when, in fact, God specifically burdens us with such a complex problem to bring us closer to awareness of worldliness within ourselves.

That is what I have discovered on my own path, which is why it struck me while reading your mes-sage—that oftentimes I was holding on to more than I realized, and that the deeper you go into Christ, it's really like peeling layers off an onion—and it's not necessarily supposed to be a wonderful experience the deeper you go.

Does that resonate with you at all? Remember that the whole point of this book is to help you faithfully walk the tension-filled line between this world and the world to come. This is where the rubber meets the road, my friends.

Are there any areas in your life where you're drifting too far, where you're motivated by worldly and selfish desires? Take a moment to really think about that. These temptations can be so subtle. My friend's words hit me like a ton of bricks, but God was again so incredibly gracious to me in allowing me to receive them. I instantly knew he was right, and I also instantly knew how "Christian" this book should be; and thus you are reading a thoroughly Christian book. Did I really believe what Jesus said? Do you?

For what does it profit a man to gain the whole world and forfeit his soul? (Mark 8:36). *No one can serve two masters, for either he will hate the one and love the other, or he will be devoted to the one and despise the other. You cannot serve God and money* (Matthew 6:24).

It was clear, at least in a practical way, that I was not living according to Jesus's teaching. I was still going after the world, albeit in a different way. Without even realizing it, I was trying to do the very thing Jesus said it was impossible to do: to have Him *and* the world. From that very moment, I was committed to writing a thoroughly Christian book, one in which I could talk about all the things I had learned about life—yet still point people to Christ and eternity. Really, it's incredible how quickly God removed the cognitive dissonance once I really started trying to be faithful. Faithfulness is always the answer.

I still hope the book does well. I don't know of anyone who sets out to publish a book that wouldn't make its way into the hands of people; but that's totally up to God. Though I will do what I can to do well here, I submit to what God has for this writing and for my life.

It needs to be said, too, that there's nothing wrong with wanting something you're pursuing to go well or even with having a lot of money. Again, nobody sets out to do something in the hope that it will fail. Our desires to do well are not inherently evil.

In fact, as Christians, we should be more passionate than anyone about doing what we do well (Ecclesiastes 9:10) since we should be doing it to the glory of God (1 Corinthians 10:31; Colossians 3:17) and since we are accountable stewards of what He has given us (Matthew 25:14). However, even as we've already considered, we must be extremely careful of our motivations and what we're truly seeking when we set out on a certain path. Are our desires pleasing to God? Are we doing what we're doing as faithful servants, or are we using God as a vehicle to bring us all our carnal desires?

But those who desire to be rich fall into temptation, into a snare, into many senseless and harmful desires that plunge people into ruin and destruction. For the love of money is a root of all kinds of evils. It is through this craving that some have wandered away from the faith and pierced themselves with many pangs. But as for you, O man of God, flee these things. Pursue righteousness, godliness, faith, love, steadfastness, gentleness. (1 Timothy 6:9–11)

Paul doesn't mince words. He never does. But what is especially striking about the above warning is verse 9. Notice that Paul is not speculating here. He doesn't say, "Those who desire to be rich *might* fall into temptation." He says that they *will* fall into temptation. It is a certainty, and this type of fall is what plunges people into ruin and destruction. Are you so arrogant as to think you know better than God, that you're stronger than He says you are? We must be so careful in these areas as we strive to do well and also live lives that are pleasing to Him.

As we noted above, our desires are not always wrong. In fact, God gives us good desires, but our hearts are deceitfully wicked (Jeremiah 17:9), and often when we think we're being faithful, we might really be drifting away from God. I hope you've seen as much from my own life. On the other hand, it's sometimes difficult to know if our motivations are ever *truly* pure. In our attempts to be faithful, we ought not to be stifled by introspection. We should examine and prepare our hearts the best we can and move forward in faith, entrusting any infirmities or imperfections to the perfect and finished work of our faithful Savior. We have to continue to go back to what we know to be true about God, ensuring that our mindset is in line with the teaching of Scripture, making it our aim to please Him in all that we do (2 Corinthians 5:9).

Make the Most Out of What You Have Been Given

As we define success and are speaking in this particular context, I also want to say that the oft-quoted sentiment that you should follow your heart and be whatever you want to be is misguided. Prudence plays here, wisdom plays, and your existing commitments play. If I want to be a teacher at a university, you might say, "Yeah, Mick, you know you're not a dumb guy. You have an articulate, albeit verbose, disposition about you. You should do that if that's what you want." But what if I said my dream was to be a starting forward for the LA Lakers or a linebacker for the Dallas Cowboys? (By the way, I'm 5'6"[ish] and about 140 pounds.) Hopefully you'd be wide-eyed and ask me if I've looked in a mirror lately. Hopefully you'd say that I probably don't even meet the height requirement to be the towel boy. You can't just go do *anything*. In order to be successful, you have to do your best to become the best you're *capable* of becoming. That means I'm never going to be in the NFL. It's just not in the cards, and I'm cool with that, by the way (1 Corinthians 7:17). Here is some more wisdom from Michael Horton:

> *In his providence, God has given to each of us specific gifts, inclinations, talents, and opportunities. We are not unlimited. Our future is not "whatever we want it to be," and we are not able to become "whatever we wish." Yet all of this is for our good—and the good of others. The gifts and opportunities we have been given are to be used not merely for private advancement, but for the public good. And this is why we all need each other.*[52]

---

52   Horton, *Ordinary*, 96.

The truth is that although we should strive to be successful, making the most out of everything God has given us, our lives are less about us than we often realize. God knows what He's doing.

Beauty in Simplicity

Such a definition of success also means that we can't just look at people and determine whether or not they're successful. It's not about money or appearance. There are a lot of people with money who are the absolute poorest of people (I know some people like this). Everyone thinks that the more things they have and the more things they achieve, the happier they'll be. This is a prevailing sentiment. J. D. Rockefeller, one of the richest men to have ever lived, was once asked how much is enough; his answer was, "Just a little bit more."[53] But we're never satisfied with the things of this world, and most people spend their whole lives seeking "just a little bit more."

There is a disdain, particularly in Western culture, for the simple, for the ordinary. But there is virtue in such things. Consider a man who works a 9 to 5 job for thirty years and supports and leads his family, raises good children, and takes a five-day vacation every year. That might be viewed as mundane by some, but that is success if that man is doing his best to become the best he's capable of becoming. A man and a woman who are married for fifty or sixty years and are faithful to each other might seem mundane to some, but that is success too. I want you to apply these axioms to your own scenarios, with your own goals, and in your own lives.

It's important to understand, commensurate with Wooden's definition of success and the teaching of Jesus, that both success and, thus, faithfulness looks different for each of us. After all, how

53 *New World Encyclopedia*, s.v. "John D. Rockefeller," https://www.newworldencyclopedia.org/entry/John_D._Rockefeller.

could we ever be considered successful if we aren't also faithful?[54] Recall that in the parable the servants were given their talents *according to their ability.* This doesn't by any means demean or denigrate those who have been given "less" in God's providence, but it again highlights the importance of being faithful with what we've been given. We need to be careful of such denigrating sentiments, even within the church.

Pay attention to the mindset of some who say things like, "Oh, well, I'm just a stay-at-home mom" or "I don't move around too well these days. All I can do is pray for people." I look at people like that and I think, what do you mean you're *just* a stay-at-home mom or you can *only* pray? We've become a people fascinated and enamored by the sensational, by the spotlight. We expect this of the world, but it ought not to be so in the church of Jesus Christ.

Again, the world views success by how famous you are or how much money you have, but we need to be careful of similar tendencies in the church as well. We tend to think that we're only being faithful to Christ or only living radically for Christ if we're on some foreign mission field risking our lives for the sake of the gospel. We think that the pastor is on some next-level tier of Christianity that the rest of us could only hope to attain. That is so wrong, though! That's not to demean the work of those in full-time vocational ministry or those risking their lives—far from it! But that is simply the place that God has called those people to. That does not at all mean that those who do more "ordinary" jobs are any less faithful to God. In fact, for many people, that is *exactly* what faithfulness is supposed to look like for them. What does faithfulness look like for you?

G. K. Chesterton said, "The most extraordinary thing in the world is an ordinary man and an ordinary woman and their ordinary children." We would do well to remember this, particularly in a culture that is overly fixated on the extraordinary. The truth

---

54   In the same sermon noted earlier, Brian Borgman, still recalling the words of Kent Hughes, says: "God's standard of success for his people...is faithfulness."

is that the men and women who have done great things for God generally didn't set out to do great things for God. They simply sought to be faithful with the opportunities God had given them. This is the kind of disposition that enables one to come to the end of life and be commended by the master: *Well done, good and faithful servant. You have been faithful over a little; I will set you over much* (Matthew 25:23).

It's faithfulness in the little things that leads to faithfulness in the big things. A friend of mine, reflecting on life, once recognized that "we often fantasize and dream of accomplishing great things, of impacting millions, of 'changing the world' while we miss the amazing opportunities and gifts staring us in the face." We tend to be worried about living mediocre lives; we tend to be worried about "settling." But as another wise friend once told me,[55] usually the things that we end up settling for are the things we should have been seeking in the first place.

As I'm writing this, I'm sitting at a Panera Bread, nearly in tears, as I observe an older man and woman sitting across from me eating lunch together. I can only assume they're married. The woman is confined to a wheelchair—permanently, it would seem—and she's having a great bit of difficulty eating her salad. Every so often her husband gently reaches over and takes her fork and puts an appropriate amount of food onto it. He also places a napkin in her hand and helps her set her cup down after she drinks. I wonder how long the two of them have been living like this.

We are sitting outside. Every so often a bit of wind kicks up, and the man reaches over and fixes his wife's hair so it isn't down over her eyes. What a beautiful picture of sacrificial love. Some might view this man's life as a waste, succumbing to the great responsibility of caring for his wife day in and day out, likely sacrificing much of his own personal gain and freedom. But I can tell you that nothing could be further from the truth, and I can tell you that the ones who view his life as a waste are the ones

---

55   I have a lot of wise friends.

who are likely wasting their lives, missing out on what is truly important. So often we think that doing something great means doing something big. This man isn't doing anything big in the sight of anyone, but I can assure you he is doing something great.

In the Gospel of Mark, we're told of a scenario in which Jesus and His disciples were walking into Capernaum (Mark 9:33–36). Jesus overheard His disciples arguing over who was the greatest among them, and when they reached the town, He asked them about it. They obviously felt a little guilty about their discussion since they kept silent when they were questioned about it (verse 34). But it's interesting that, much like we've done in this chapter, Jesus's correction amounted to informing them about a proper understanding of what it means to be great. He didn't say, "Don't be great!" Rather, Jesus recognized that the way His disciples understood greatness was a bit off, and He said to them, *If anyone would be first, he must be last of all and servant of all* (verse 35).

So be great, but make sure you're great in the eyes of God and not in the eyes of the world, *for what is exalted among men is an abomination in the sight of God* (Luke 16:15).

Journey well.

CHAPTER 9:
You're Going to Die

*Your days are numbered. Use them to throw open
the windows of your soul to the sun. If you do
not, the sun will soon set, and you with it.*
— MARCUS AURELIUS

You're going to die. Indeed, the results are in of a new survey that was recently conducted, and top scientists have found that ten out of ten people eventually die. I'll stop jesting now. Death is a serious thing. Perhaps in some way you've been touched by it already. Perhaps you've lost a loved one or a dear friend. Perhaps you've had a near-death experience or are even now battling a potentially devastating condition. Or maybe you're simply afraid to die. Death is something we all must face. God's Word teaches that *it is appointed for man to die once, and after that comes judgment* (Hebrews 9:27).

Charles Spurgeon, the "Prince of Preachers," said, "Men have been helped to live by remembering that they must die."[56] Consistent

---

56   Charles Spurgeon, "What Is Your Life?" (sermon, Metropolitan Tabernacle, Newington, March 30, 1884), https://www.spurgeongems.org/sermon/chs1773.pdf.

with what we've said about living in light of God's truth, we must especially consider the reality of death and be deliberate in allowing it to inform how we live. The interesting thing is that most people tend to live opposite of that. Most people do everything they can to avoid the very thought of death—ignoring it and suppressing it until it catches them unawares. I suppose most probably do this out of fear. Do you fear death?

A friend once reminded me that "Christians are called to live as those who have conquered the fear of death. Our Lord has freed us from the slavery to such fear, and through His victorious conquest has enabled us to live lives of unwavering fidelity to Him" (Hebrews 2:14–15). Although the focus of this chapter—death—is a biblical and beneficial one (Ecclesiastes 7:2), we must remember that Jesus has defeated death, and we have joined Him in that victory. Our view of death, then, is not the same as the world's.

Christ's resurrection neutralizes the otherwise dominating rule of life's old enemy. Death is not the final word. As Christ has been raised, so, too, will we be raised (2 Corinthians 4:14). This truth is why we don't have to try to save our lives. We aren't going to lose them! This is why we can live fearlessly and faithfully. This is also ultimately why we can step beyond our comfort zones without worrying. We aren't here to preserve our lives! We are here to live them and honor God through them.

This is a great difficulty in the Christian life, though, and I'll tell you that I struggle with it sometimes. Death can be a fearful thing. It's a sobering thing. And although, as Christians, we ought to be thinking of death differently than unbelievers, it's still an enemy. It is still *unnatural*, though it is part of our *natural* world. What I mean is that God didn't create the world with death as a part of it. It's not natural in that way, and yet having only lived in a post-fall world, it seems quite natural to us. Nevertheless, death is widely considered a negative occurrence, even though it's the door we must pass through to meet our Lord—unless He comes back before we die.

Leaving Our Legacy

In considering death, we need to allow it to inform how we live in the here and now, and we need to live in light of the fact that death is only the beginning in many ways. All of us have an eternity before us, a forever to look forward to, and though salvation is by grace, there's a sense in which what we do now will be determinative of our eternal future. But how should it inform how we live? For one thing, it puts things in perspective for us. The right view of death allows us to major in the majors and minor in the minors. It helps us live for the things that are truly important. Mark Manson says:

> *Confronting the reality of our own mortality is important because it obliterates all the crappy, fragile, superficial values in life. While most people whittle their days chasing another buck, or a little bit more fame and attention, or a little bit more assurance that they're right or loved, death confronts all of us with a far more important question: What is your legacy?*
>
> *How will the world be different and better when you're gone? What mark will you have made? What influence will you have caused? They say that a butterfly flapping its wings in Africa can cause a hurricane in Florida; well, what hurricanes will you leave in your wake?*[57]

Manson is right, of course, but he stops short of a crucial point, and his statement needs clarification. We need to apply what we've already considered as we think about our "legacy." Our legacy can be anything that glorifies God. Remember, this is going to look different for each of us. Some of us will preach the

---

57   Manson, *The Subtle Art*, 205.

gospel to hundreds or thousands of people, some of us will raise up families in the fear of the Lord, and some of us will simply seek to be a blessing to those around us and give as we are able to our local church. There is no perfect picture of how this looks, but the question is, What are you living for? Are you building your legacy with gold, silver, and precious stones? Or are you building it out of things that are worthless and whose end is to be burned (1 Corinthians 3:12–15)?

Additionally, Manson's philosophy falls short in that he fails to recognize the importance of being made right with God through Christ and living in a way that is aligned with that reality. Legacy is important, yes; but the more important question is what does God think of your legacy? Even if you send all your kids to college or build an orphanage—all good things—what does that matter if you die and go to hell? In a temporal sense, it matters, of course. Non-believers do a lot of good things for the common kingdom[58] (Luke 6:33), and we should all be about doing good for those around us—whether it is in a specifically Christian context or not.

Temporal Actions

Jesus tells us to engage in business until He comes (Luke 19:13), which implies that our temporal actions do matter. We should care about life this side of eternity. We are to mirror the exiles in Babylon. They were told to build houses, to take wives, and to have children. They were commanded to multiply and prosper. They were told to seek the welfare of the city where the Lord had sent them into exile (Jeremiah 29:4–7). We are ourselves exiles (Hebrews 11:13; 1 Peter 1:17; 2:11). This is not our home, yet we are not to be idle.

---

58   Terminology taken from David VanDrunen, *Living in God's Two Kingdoms: A Biblical Vision for Christianity and Culture* (Wheaton, IL: Crossway Books, 2010).

We ought not view temporal endeavors as simply rearranging the furniture on the *Titanic*. Rather, we should live in such a way that allows our light to shine before the world and causes people to ask us for a reason for the hope that is within us (Matthew 5:14–16; 1 Peter 3:15). So I ask again: What are you living for?

One of the most life-changing books I've read is a short treatise by the philosopher Seneca titled *On the Shortness of Life*. Like all non-Christian philosophers, he stops short of ultimate truth; nevertheless, he gets a lot right, and I was extremely sobered by his thoughts. The thrust of his treatise is basically that despite the common notion that life is too short, it actually is not. Here is what Seneca says:

> *It is not that we have such a short space of time, but that we waste much of it. Life is long enough, and it has been given in sufficiently generous measure to allow the accomplishment of the very greatest things if the whole of it is well invested. But when it is squandered in luxury and carelessness, when it is devoted to no good end, forced at last by the ultimate necessity, we perceive that it has passed away before we were aware that it was passing. So it is—the life we receive is not short, but we make it so, nor do we have any lack of it, but are wasteful of it. Just as great and princely wealth is scattered in a moment when it comes into the hands of a bad owner, while wealth however limited, if it is entrusted to a good guardian, increases by use, so our life is amply long for him who orders it properly.*[59]

Obviously, we need to consider Seneca's words as a general principle, for it is indeed a sad reality that many in this world do die

---

59   Lucius Seneca, *On the Shortness of Life*, trans. John W. Basore (UK: Vigeo Press, 2016), 2.

untimely deaths. I once read that getting old is a privilege denied to many. That's so true! But I've come to agree with Seneca. The time on this earth that most people are given really is sufficient to accomplish a great deal. Just look at the lives of those who have. I've stopped saying that life is too short. Instead, I recognize that it is *quick* and that I have to be grateful for and maximize every moment I'm given here. This is hard, but it is necessary if we are to be faithful stewards of the lives we've been given. The quickness of life is a biblical concept: *You do not know what tomorrow will bring. What is your life? For you are a mist that appears for a little time and then vanishes* (James 4:14).

We need to recognize this and live accordingly.

Living in the Now

On January 24, 2019 at around 1:30 in the afternoon, I called St. Elizabeth's Hospital to get an update on the condition of my dad. He had been there a day or so at that point, but he had been in and out of hospitals and rehab facilities and the like for the past six months, so all this had become pretty commonplace.

The nurse I spoke with gave a positive report and asked me if I wanted to be connected to his room to talk with him. I told him no because I planned on talking with my dad when I went to visit. At about 5:30 that same evening, I had just gotten home from work and was letting my dog out when I received a phone call from the hospital saying my dad was unresponsive. I don't think the weight of what that meant sunk in right away. In fact, I don't think it sank in at all until I arrived at the hospital and the nurse told me that he had passed. He was sixty-seven.

I remember my heart dropping when the nurse, trying to give me a report as to what the situation was, finally finished her thought and confirmed the worst. It seems that I should have let the first nurse connect me to my dad's room earlier so I could have talked with him one last time. Now I would never talk to him again. If I would have known that I would never speak with him again, I certainly would have valued the time I did speak with him much more. I would have considered visiting him less burdensome than it sometimes seemed. I would have taken more interest in the things he had to share. I would have told him how much I appreciated him.

That is the nature of life and death, though. We just don't know. The time I had with my dad went so quickly. I had plenty of time to spend with him—more than thirty years. That's a lot of time when you think about it. But it went by so quickly, and I didn't realize just how quickly—until it was too late. This is why Seneca's words are so important; this is why God's words are so important. And this is why ordering our lives according to these truths is so very important.

Seneca also caused me to realize one of the great plights of all mankind—and that is not living in the moment, not living in the *now*. That seems a bit cliché, but it's necessary if we are to fully enjoy this life and make full use of what we've been given. It's so difficult to live in the now, though. We're always looking forward to something else. That's not necessarily a bad thing in and of itself either. We might have vacations planned that we're looking forward to, we might be looking forward to having our own family one day, or perhaps next week an old friend is coming to visit. Those are all good things to be excited for, but that excitement becomes bad when we're excited for such things at the expense of what we should be doing in the now. This is especially true when we stop and consider that we aren't promised tomorrow (James 4:13-14).

So I want you to consider your life. I want you to consider the things you're involved in and the direction you're moving. Is your focus where it should be? When it should be? Upon what it should be? Are your endeavors worthy? Are they pleasing to the Lord? Or are you squandering what you have been given, wasting it as a great inheritance might be foolishly spent in a moment, like a foolish servant who buries what his master gave him in the ground (Matthew 25:18)?

Have you ever been on a road trip or an airplane ride or maybe just driving home from work—and suddenly, without realizing it, your trip is over? You've arrived at your destination. You exclaim, "Wow, here already!" You hadn't even been aware of the time that passed because you were so otherwise distracted.[60] We've all been there. Think about that feeling. That's how most people go through life. As Seneca wrote, "[One] finds that he has reached the end of his journey before he was aware he was approaching it."[61]

This happens because we don't live in the now. It happens because our minds are distracted, always someplace other than where they should be. It's tough to remember exactly what I was thinking, but I'm sure that for more than some of those visits with my dad, I was thinking of being somewhere else. Maybe I was thinking of how I could make an efficient exit without being a jerk (and sometimes just straight up being a jerk). And don't even get me started on our cell phones. We are distracted. We don't live in the now.

Really Living

Oftentimes we don't actually live at all; we simply exist. We're just here killing time and stealing oxygen. Even those who are older might be wrinkled and gray, but their appearance is no indication that they've lived long. Seneca observed this and likened it to a man leaving on a ship for a voyage and being caught up and tossed about by a storm. Such a man is moved here and there by the wind, but he's just going in circles. "Not much voyaging does he have, but much tossing about."[62] Seneca says, "The majority of mortals complain bitterly of the spitefulness of Nature, because we are born for a brief span of life, because even this space that has been granted to us rushes by so speedily and so swiftly that

---

60   Seneca, Shortness, 18. I used Seneca's thought process here, though I changed it slightly.

61   Seneca, *Shortness*, 18.

62   Seneca, *Shortness*, 14.

*all save a very few find life at an end just when they are getting ready
to live*"[63] (emphasis added).

I don't want that to happen to you. Oh, that you would consider
these words and be spared of such an end! We need to keep these
important truths ever at the front of our minds. We need to live
the life we've been given, not waste it.

Les Brown recounts the words of Dr. Howard Thurman, a
mentor of Dr. Martin Luther King Jr.:

> *The ideal situation for a man or woman to die is
> to have family members praying with them as they
> cross over. But imagine, if you will, being on your
> deathbed, and standing around your bed [are] the
> ghost[s] of the dreams, the ideas, the abilities given
> to you... but you, for whatever reason, you never
> pursued those dreams, you never acted on those ideas,
> you never used those gifts and there they are looking
> at you with large, angry eyes saying, "We came to you,
> and only you could have given us life, and now we
> must die with you forever.*"[64]

I don't know about you, but a lot of angry things would be
standing around my bed. Such a picture should cause us to take
an inventory of the things we've been pushing off and the things
we've been neglecting. It should cause us to really assess what
God would have us do here, how He would have us spend our
lives—the *one* life we've been given. This is a sobering statement,
but again, I believe it falls short of the truth that the Christian
must recognize, a truth that all people will face whether they now
recognize it or not.

---

63   Seneca, 1.

64   Les Brown, "Les Brown's 7 Rules for Success! You Have Greatness
Within You!," https://www.youtube.com/watch?v=Sdktvc1vKR8.

We will, all of us, stand before the judgment seat of God and give an account for our lives (Romans 14:10–12). We will have to explain to God why we didn't make use of what He saw fit to give us (Matthew 25:19, 24–25). Whatever our explanation might be on that day, I trust it will be found wanting. So although we recognize the importance of all these temporal concerns, the Christian must live his or her life *coram Deo*—before the face of God. He sees everything (Hebrews 4:13), He knows everything (1 John 3:20), and we should want to honor Him in all that we do (2 Corinthians 5:9).

We have continually referenced the parable of the talents (Matthew 25:14–30). It teaches us many valuable lessons about life, and I want us to once more consider what the master said to the servants who were faithful with what was given to them. *His master said to him, "Well done, good and faithful servant. You have been faithful over a little; I will set you over much. Enter into the joy of your master"* (Matthew 25:21).

What could be more important to any of us than to hear Jesus speak those words? We need to live our lives in the hopeful expectation of one day standing before our Lord and being told, "Well done." The apostle Paul fully expected that, and it was undoubtedly a powerful motivation for him to run the race and fight the good fight until the very end (2 Timothy 4:6–8).

Putting God First

For all of the great things that God has given us in this life, we need to be putting Him first (Matthew 6:33). We need to guard our hearts against the things of this world (Proverbs 4:23; 1 John 2:15–17) and ensure that we are worshiping the Giver and not His gifts (Romans 1:25). These are things that are true of every Christian.

Christians have been called out of darkness and into His marvelous light (1 Peter 2:9), but the transforming power of the gospel is such that if the work in our hearts is genuine, we aren't just enlightened people walking around living the same lives we used to. We're completely new creatures (2 Corinthians 5:17). Christ died *that we might die to sin and live to righteousness* (1 Peter 2:24). Is it plausible, for even one second, to think that Christ's death effectually applied to the life of a sinner will fail to accomplish the purpose for which it was given? Not even close!

This means that if we are His, if we are truly walking in the light, we are going to be living differently—not perfectly, but differently. Our desires will be different, our behaviors will be different, and the way we see the world and the way we want to see the world will be different. Everything will be different. Are you different?

There's nothing more important than the condition of your eternal soul. If you haven't come to a place where you're trusting in Christ as your only hope of salvation and are daily repenting of your sins, then you need to really prioritize things in your life.

Stop reading this book and cry out to God immediately! Ask Him for forgiveness. Ask Him to change you. Ask Him to give you a new heart. Christ is a mighty Savior, and there is no sin too great for Him to forgive, no burden too heavy for Him to bear. Put your hope in Him. You will not be disappointed (Romans 10:11). Go to Him now! He promises that whoever goes to Him, He will never cast out (John 6:37).

Remember, too, that it is the kindness of God that leads us to repentance (Romans 2:4). Have you ever stopped to think about just how kind God has been to you? Even if you've been through some difficulties, I know you can recognize His kindness in your life. *He has shown kindness by giving you rain from heaven and crops in their seasons; he provides you with plenty of food and fills your hearts with joy* (Acts 14:17 NIV). *He himself gives to all mankind life and breath and everything* (Acts 17:25), and above all He has given us His Son (John 3:16; Romans 8:32). Consider, then, this kind God and go to Him. Spend your life seeking to glorify Him. He is worthy!

In Christ, we are brought to a place where we can approach God, be declared right before Him, and have a relationship with

Him—seeing and enjoying His presence in every part of our lives.[65] This is the gospel. This is the good news. Salvation cannot be earned. We are saved by grace alone, through faith alone, in Christ alone. Nothing we do, no legacy we leave behind, is going to make us right before God or give meaning to life apart from God. But we can rejoice that our loving Father sent His only son to die on our behalf and that whoever believes in Him will have eternal life (John 3:16).

To close out this chapter and this very important topic of living in light of death, I want to share one of my favorite poems with you. It was quoted in a sermon by Leonard Ravenhill[66] and is called "A Hundred Years From Now" by Walden Parker. It is beautifully illustrative of much that we've been discussing:

> *It will not make much difference, friend,*
> *A hundred years from now,*
> *If you live in a stately mansion*
> *Or on a floating river scow;*
> *If the clothes you wear are tailor-made*
> *Or pieced together somehow,*
> *If you eat big steaks or beans and cakes*
> *A hundred years from now.*
>
> *It won't matter about your bank account*
> *Or the make of car you drive,*
> *For the grave will claim your riches and fame*
> *And the things for which you strive.*
> *There's a deadline that we all must meet*
> *And no one will be late.*
> *It won't matter then all the places you've been,*
> *Each one will keep that date.*

---

65   For more on this, see Tim Chester's book *Enjoying God*. Other than the Bible, it may be the most important and most life-changing book I've read.

66   Leonard Ravenhill, "Something Is Missing in the Church," https://www.youtube.com/watch?v=IKmEdwbhers.

We will only have in eternity
What we gave away on earth;
When we go to the grave we can only save
The things of eternal worth.
What matters, friend, the earthly gain
For which some men always bow?
For your destiny will be sealed, you see—
A hundred years from now.

As we consider all these things, we need to understand that the reality of both our mortality and our relationship with Christ necessarily informs the way that we live. This means we must seek to honor Him in everything we do (1 Corinthians 10:31; 2 Corinthians 5:9). It means that if we attain a certain measure of wealth or success, we must view it as God would view it. We must not act like the rich fool, seeking after wealth only so we can build bigger barns to selfishly hoard it all (Luke 12:13–21). Instead, we should labor after the food that does not perish (John 6:27) and lay our treasure up in heaven (Matthew 6:20). Remember, it's not wrong to have the things of this world, but we must ensure that the things of this world do not have us.[67] Jesus said, *Where your treasure is, there your heart will be also* (Matthew 6:21). We must ensure that in all our endeavors, our heart is a heart for God. The reality of our relationship with Christ informs the necessity of this, while the reality of our mortality informs the urgency of it.

An awareness of one's life passing before them, coupled with the reality of one's death looming over them, forms an interesting and unique perspective for the Christian. God is glorified in us "living in the now." He is glorified in our enjoyment of the creation He Himself has given us to enjoy. He is glorified in us living life to the fullest (Ecclesiastes 9:10) and making the most of our time (Ephesians 5:15–16)—when we do those things His way. But at the same time,

---

67   David Garland, *1 Corinthians*, Baker Exegetical Commentary on the New Testament (Grand Rapids: Baker Academic, 2003), 330.

we recognize that this is not our home (Hebrews 13:14) and that our time here is temporary (1 Peter 1:24), even fleeting (James 4:14). We are aliens and sojourners here (1 Peter 2:11). Indeed, *here we have no lasting city, but we seek the city that is to come* (Hebrews 13:14).

Our view of this life, then, is not one of "Eat, drink, and be merry, for tomorrow we die" (Luke 12:19; 1 Corinthians 15:32). Although such a perspective recognizes the reality of enjoying our lives now in light of our mortality, it does so completely outside of the framework we've spent so much time establishing, and that makes all the difference in the world. We need to put on our Bible-tinted glasses. We ought to be enjoying what we can in full recognition that it won't last, but we ought to do so thankfully and in a way that doesn't find the meaning of our existence in the things of this world. David Gibson, citing Iain Provan's commentary on Ecclesiastes as the source for his insight, writes about this: "Death can radically enable us to enjoy life. By relativizing all that we do in our days under the sun, death can change us from people who want to control life for gain into people who find deep joy in receiving life as a gift. This is the main message of [the book of] Ecclesiastes in a nutshell: *life in God's world is gift, not gain.*"[68]

Gibson concludes: "It is so striking that while Ecclesiastes tells us there is no 'gain' to be had under the sun, the apostle Paul says that there is in fact one thing to gain: dying. 'For to me to live is Christ, and to die is gain' (Philippians 1:21). Paul knew that in Christ, living and dying mean win-win. We can labor for Christ while we live, and we can live with Christ when we die."[69] So enjoy the gift that God has given you—the gift of life and all that comes with it. But never lose sight of what is truly gain.

"For your destiny will be sealed, you see—a hundred years from now."

Journey well.

---

68   David Gibson, *Living Life Backward: How Ecclesiastes Teaches Us to Live in Light of the End* (Wheaton, IL: Crossway, 2017), 37.

69   Gibson, 162.

Conclusion

To each there comes in their lifetime a special moment when they are figuratively tapped on the shoulder and offered the chance to do a very special thing, unique to them and fitted to their talents. What a tragedy if that moment finds them unprepared or unqualified for that which could have been their finest hour.
—WINSTON S. CHURCHILL

Well, it appears we've nearly reached the end of our journey—at least our journey through this book together. My hope is that your journey is just beginning, or beginning anew, after taking in all that I've shared in the preceding pages. I really want to encourage you one last time to take what I've said to heart. The lessons and wisdom I've shared with you took me the better part of a decade to learn. What a tremendous blessing books can be! You're holding about ten years of my life in your hand. Put it to good use! Don't be like the fool in Proverbs 5 who groaned at the end of his life (verse 11) because he did not listen to the voice of his teachers or incline his ear to his instructors (verse 13).

As you've seen, my aim has been to spare you from foolish mistakes, as well as to prepare you for some of the things in life that most people don't like to talk about. In Hosea 4:6, God says, *My people are destroyed for lack of knowledge.* What a tragedy! All of these things I've shared with you are things I wish someone would have told me a long time ago and things I wish I would have paid more attention to. I've written this book so you don't have to say that. If, like me, you're coming to an awareness of these things a bit later in life, don't be discouraged. It's never too late to make a change.

Looking back on all that we've considered, you can see that we've walked a pretty dangerous line—the line between living for eternity and living well in the present. If we perfectly understood all that God said about living in this world in a way that honors Him, and if our hearts weren't bent in the direction of sin, it wouldn't be such a dangerous line. But we are fallen sinners, and we are tempted to be pulled into the mire of this world more often than we'd like to admit. Thus, it is crucial to always be looking through our Bible-tinted glasses.

We need to see things as they really are because the way they look at first glance isn't always the reality. Proverbs 5 shows us how deceptive such things can be in how the adulterous woman is described there. We are told that her lips drip honey and her speech is smoother than oil (verse 3), but in reality, in the end, she is as bitter as wormwood (verse 4),[70] and her steps follow the path to the grave (verse 5). Solomon here recognizes the alluring appearance of such things—things that look like they will be pleasing, but that will actually kill us.

The same type of deception can be seen all the way back in the garden of Eden. We're told that *the woman saw that the tree was good for food, and that it was a delight to the eyes* (Genesis 3:6). Clearly, Eve did not have her Bible-tinted glasses on. She should have looked at that fruit and gone in the opposite direction. It should not have appeared good to her. God had explicitly com-

---

70   Wormwood is "a bitter, oil-yielding plant, symbolic of suffering." Joel Beeke, *The Reformation Heritage KJV Study Bible* (Grand Rapids: Reformation Heritage Books, 2014), 891.

manded not to eat of that tree![71] In her mind, eating of that tree should have been equated with drinking hemlock![72] But we all know how that story ended—the entire creation, Adam, and his entire progeny were plunged into a curse—all because of sin.

Tragically, we have our own little stories every day that end the same way. We often forget to put our glasses on, and thus we sin against God, go the wrong way, and do the wrong thing. This is why we need to be reminded of all these things so often (2 Peter 1:13; 3:1). We are a forgetful people with wandering eyes and wandering appetites (Jeremiah 2:32).

Such a reality leads us right back to the cross, though. It leads us right back to praising the God who has made us and saved us. We serve a God who, when we forget our glasses, or straight up choose not to wear them, never lets us walk around blindly for too long. Genesis 3:15, the first gospel promise in the Scriptures, is right on the heels of that first sin in the garden, and in the same way, the grace of God is right on the heels of all of His wandering sheep. Even as Paul said, where sin abounds, grace abounds all the more (Romans 5:20).

It is in light of that grace that I exhort you to move immediately forward to the glory of God. Question one of the Westminster Shorter Catechism asks, "What is the chief end of man?" It answers, "To glorify God and to enjoy Him forever." Whatever endeavors we pursue in this life, whatever blessings God chooses to bestow upon us, we are to glorify Him in them, keeping our eye on the eternity that we will spend enjoying Him. Enjoying Him now through His gifts, His promises, and His Word is but a taste of the joy we will have in eternity when we see Him face to face (1 Corinthians 13:12).

As we traveled through this book, we discussed a lot. We walked through all kinds of real-world topics that I know you'll

---

71 I first heard this explained about ten years ago in a lecture by Dr. Richard Gamble at Reformed Presbyterian Theological Seminary.

72 Hemlock is a poisonous plant.

encounter in your life in one way or another. We talked about the importance of having a proper biblical mindset and how that is foundational to living faithfully. We talked about rejection and disappointment. We considered a proper view of success and living in light of our death. Over and over again, we considered the fact that everything God has given us is a stewardship with which He has entrusted us and for which we will be held accountable. We talked about planning, getting out of the comfort zone, taking action, and persevering. There's a lot there!

So how do we put all this together? How can we summarize the proper way to traverse that fine line we mentioned at the outset? How can we live wisely and well, enjoying the life that God gives us, while still recognizing that this is not our home? How are we to view our life, the world around us, and our involvement in it? The apostle Paul makes reference to this very thing in his first letter to the church at Corinth:

> *This is what I mean, brothers: the appointed time has grown very short. From now on, let those who have wives live as though they had none, and those who mourn as though they were not mourning, and those who rejoice as though they were not rejoicing, and those who buy as though they had no goods, and those who deal with the world as though they had no dealings with it. For the present form of this world is passing away. (1 Corinthians 7:29–31)*

At first glance, this might seem a little confusing, but let's break it down and see what Paul is telling us. First off, he tells us that *the time has grown very short.* Before you get all hung up on that statement, you need to understand that contextually "Paul is not concerned about the *duration* of time; but the *character* of the time. He is talking not about how little time is left but about how Christ's death and resurrection have changed how Christians should look at the time that is left" (emphasis added).[73] Isn't that what we've been saying this whole time? Remember, right belief begets right practice. What we know to be true about ourselves, Christ, and this present world necessarily informs how we live.

David Garland writes, "Christians stand on a mountaintop, as it were.... From this vantage point, they can see the termination of history on earth and its goal. They can discern what really matters, and they should conduct their lives accordingly."[74] Paul is saying, among other things, that "time is at a premium."[75]

Didn't we say that Christians should be the most passionate and committed people of all in this life? We know that things here are temporary—fleeting. Therefore, we enjoy all the more what God gives us; and this same truth that motivates us to be passionate in our earthly endeavors compels us not to be overly invested in temporal things—they are temporary—fleeting. "Christians should see and judge more clearly what is and what is not important."[76]

The examples that Paul uses all work to demonstrate a central principle that basically amounts to that age-old saying of "We are to be in the world, but not of the world." In mentioning marriage here, Paul is not weighing in on the various considerations one might have when thinking about marriage. He does that in this very chapter in the verses surrounding this passage. Rather, as Garland quotes from James Moffatt, this "is a passionate, heroic reminder that the Christian life must never be identified with even the nearest and dearest of worldly experiences, however legitimate and appealing they may be."[77] Paul is not saying not to get married; he's just saying to make sure you have a right view of marriage and to make sure you're holding it in its proper place.

---

73   David Garland, *1 Corinthians*, 328–329.
74   Garland, 329.
75   Garland, 328.
76   Garland, 329.
77   Garland, 329.

Again, this is exactly what we've been saying about life here in the present all along.

Paul mentions mourning and rejoicing as well. Just like when he mentions marriage, he's not saying that such things aren't going to happen or that we shouldn't be a part of them. In fact, just as in every example he gives here, he presupposes that all these things *will* be happening. "His point is that laughter and tears are not the last word. Christians should never allow themselves 'to be lost in either.'"[78]

Lastly, Paul talks about buying and possessing worldly things and dealing with the world. He again presupposes that we will be involved with the world. We are not to shut ourselves off from it or attempt to live in a vacuum. Again, the point here is that we are to have a proper understanding of our place in this world as Christians, which is really the key to living wisely, well, and faithfully in the present. To quote David Garland at length:

> *[Paul] knows that the Christian's well-being does not depend on cleverly taking advantage of the world's opportunities and becoming "successful" according to the world's standards. Being engaged with the world is one thing; becoming enmeshed in it is another. Becoming wrapped up in the world is to become wrapped up in a death shroud. One can continue to buy, sell, and marry—in sum, to use this world—but one must recognize that the things of this world are short-lived. He exhorts the Corinthians never to get so lost in the things of the world that they lose sight of this conviction. The world should never be the means whereby persons attempt to create and define their lives.*
>
> *What, then, does Paul recommend? He does not advocate indifference to the world or flight from it (cf. 2*

---

78   Garland, 330.

Thess. 3:12). He does not demonize the world as evil, since the "as nots" presuppose involvement in the world. What these "as nots" do is pose a question: What is it that molds one's life? Since the world is not the source of Christians' life or the ground of their hope, they should not allow it to cast them in the forge of its deadly furnace. He warns against the danger of "the world's power to entangle and disarm, to make one less ready for the imminent End." The "as nots" require Christians to detach themselves from the norms because an "alternative world" exists that offers a different way of living governed by a completely different set of values. They are to live in this earthbound world, with its many gods and lords, as those who belong to another, eternal world (Phil. 3:20) and to the one God and one Lord [1 Cor. 8:5–6]. The "as nots" are a rhetorically more dashing way of saying, "Do not be conformed to this world" (Rom. 12:2).[79]

As you can see, in Paul's way of thinking, the reality of this present world passing away informs how he instructs us to live. He doesn't say, "Don't live." That would be kind of an odd thing to say, but he does tell us to live a certain way, a way that is quite different from the rest of the world, a way that is impacted by knowing who God is and who we are in Him. In short, Paul is saying, "Live, but let your ultimate disposition be one of temperance, of sobriety;[80] even in the midst of your most passionate pursuits, let your actions be informed by the eternal truths of God's Word and the temporary nature of all that composes this present world."

---

79 Garland, 331. Note: I excluded Garland's parenthetical references to avoid distraction.

80 The New Testament is replete with exhortations to be sober-minded: 1 Thessalonians 5:6, 8; 1 Timothy 3:2, 11; 2 Timothy 4:5; Titus 2:2; 1 Peter 1:13; 4:7; 5:8.

The Christian life, then, is a paradox. The Christian is the one who should be most passionate about the things of this life, motivated by the urgency of mortality (Ecclesiastes 9:10) and the reality that everything he has been given is a gift and a stewardship from God (Matthew 25:14–30; 1 Timothy 4:4–5). Yet he is also the most willing to part with those things because he recognizes that his citizenship is in heaven (Philippians 3:20). The Christian is, therefore, the most invested and the least invested person in this world at the same time. He walks a dangerous line.

Paul's words here in this passage tell us how we put everything together that we've been discussing. They tell us how we live in this present age wisely, well, and faithfully, balancing that line of enjoying life in the present, living life to the fullest, and still looking to eternity. Whew! That's a lot to take in. And if you still feel a little unresolved in the tension, that's okay. In discussing the tensions of Scripture, sometimes I feel like a Ping-Pong ball being bounced from one side of a particular spectrum to the other, never quite sure where to find the equilibrium. But God has created us to live in this tension, to rest in this tension, and to trust Him through this tension.

Even though Paul basically sums up everything we've been considering in a couple verses, it's still pretty heavy stuff! So now you know how to live. But (don't worry—we're almost done) if you're like me, you recognize that there's a question that's kind of begged here, and it's kind of an important one. Now you know the *how*, but do you know the *what*? *What* are you supposed to do now? Seriously, that's the burning question, right? Well, I'll leave you (yes, leave you, as in we're done here; I told you we were almost finished) with a short story from my friend Jeff (you know—the dear and eccentric friend I mentioned earlier).

There was a time (many years ago now) when my hometown of Youngstown was a real hustling and bustling kind of place. During those days, there was no shortage of successful businessmen and the like who headquartered their empires within the city. Well, my friend Jeff, never being the shy or timid one, decided he was going to approach one of these successful men and find out what made him tick and what he needed to do in order to be successful himself. So Jeff did what was necessary and made an appointment with Mr. Mirto, the chairman of a company called Rhiel Supply.

On the day of his appointment, Jeff showed up at Mr. Mirto's office, and you can kind of picture how a scene like that would play out. This young kid enters into a regal-looking reception room where the secretary was likely eyeing him incredulously.

"How can I help you?" she asked.

"I'm here to see Mr. Mirto."

It was very likely that she doubted the authenticity of such a statement, but after checking the books, she confirmed such and instructed him to sit down and wait until he was summoned. When you go into a place like that, you aren't simply called; you're summoned. Eventually Jeff was led back to Mr. Mirto's office. There was Mr. Mirto in a three-piece suit, sitting in a high-back chair, looking every bit of the part.

"What can I do for you?" he asked.

"Well, sir, it's no secret that you're a pretty successful guy. You run this company and you are known and respected throughout the community. You seem to be living the life you want to live, and I was just wondering what you need to do in order to be successful. What do I need to do to be successful?"

Mr. Mirto looked at him plainly for a few seconds, and his answer was quick, short, and final.

He answered, "Do something. Now get out of here."

"Do something." At first you might be inclined to think that's kind of a cop-out answer. "Do something." What help is that? All that effort on Jeff's part for just two words? The guy wasn't much help at all! Well, you might be thinking that way, but if you think a little harder, I think you'll see that the advice is really quite fitting, and it's what I will leave you with.

Do something.

Once again we'll ask, "Is youth wasted on the young?" I think we still have to answer the same way. Generally, it is—but it doesn't have to be that way. It doesn't have to be that way with you.

I don't know what God has called you to in this life. Maybe you don't even know yet, but figure it out and then do it, and don't do it like the world does it. Do it as you apply all the principles we've been discussing in this book. Do it to the glory of God. Do it *now*!

Do something.

> *The end of the matter; all has been heard. Fear God and keep his commandments, for this is the whole duty of man. For God will bring every deed into judgment, with every secret thing, whether good or evil. (Ecclesiastes 12:13–14)*

Journey well.

Thank you for reading my book!

I hope everything I've shared proves to be helpful to you.

I'd love to know what you thought of the book, and I'd be grateful if you could take a quick moment to leave me a review on Amazon.

Thanks again!

Journey well.

—Mick

Made in the USA
Las Vegas, NV
29 October 2021

33307648R00083